To   Dear Dad

With very much
Love

Maddy & Paul

x x x
x x
x

SONG BIRDS

SONG BIRDS

BY

PERCY EDWARDS

ILLUSTRATED BY

RAYMOND

WATSON

1986

THE HERBERT PRESS

© Copyright 1986 Percy Edwards
© Copyright 1986 Illustrations: Raymond Watson

First published in Great Britain 1986
by The Herbert Press Limited
46 Northchurch Road, London N1 4EJ

Edited and designed by John Hadfield
Typeset by Butler & Tanner Ltd, Frome, Somerset
Printed and bound in Hong Kong by
South China Printing Co.

British Library Cataloguing in Publication Data:

Edwards, Percy
    Song birds.
    1. Passeriformes   2. Birds—Europe
    I.Title   II. Watson, Raymond
    598.8'094   QL696.P2

ISBN 0-906969-58-1

THE CONTENTS

INTRODUCTION

The wild-life of Britain, as distinct from man's handiwork in the landscape, is increasingly recognized as a most precious part of our national inheritance. But have you realized that for the most part, whether it be meadows, mountains or rivers, trees or flowers, animals or even insects such as butterflies, nearly all wild-life is something that we enjoy with our eyes? But there is one aspect of nature that we are aware of through our ears: that is the songs of birds.

Anyone who looks through Raymond Watson's marvellous illustrations to this book will recognize that most birds are also beautiful to look at; but their unique contribution to our delight is their music. It is hardly surprising that bird song has always been a favourite theme of English poets.

Bird song has meant more than anything else for me during over seventy years of a happy life, spent almost entirely in the county of my birthplace, Suffolk. At the age of eight one of my elder brothers took me onto Rushmere Heath, just outside Ipswich, and it was there, during what we now call the Kaiser's War, that I was lying under the trees when I became aware of a bird above me calling out something that sounded just like '*Mary-Mary!*' Suddenly, it seemed, my ears were opened and I felt I must somehow answer that bird in his own tongue, so I pursed my mouth and attempted a few sounds of mimicry. After a while I heard the faint cry again, '*Mary-Mary!*' I heard him singing several times after that, but I didn't see him for about three weeks, and then when I called to him he swooped towards me, the bright yellow bars of his outstretched wings flashing, and landed on a low branch, staring at me, and anxiously calling '*Mary-Mary!*'.

I didn't know it then, but he saw me as an intruder on his territory, and was trying to drive me off. A soldier whom I knew slightly told me the bird was a Siskin. Later another soldier told me it was not a Siskin; it was a Draw-water. He explained that a Draw-water looked rather like a Siskin, but Siskins only came to Suffolk in the winter. That was my first lesson in ornithology. From then on I read every book about birds that I could lay my hands on, and one of the first things I learnt was that 'draw-water' was a Suffolk name for a Greenfinch, which is not unlike a Siskin, though lacking the dark marking.

When I was in my teens I realized that the Almighty had given me an unusual faculty for the use of my lungs, throat and lips. It was not until some years later that a famous old entertainer called Charles Coborn, having heard me exercising my modest talents at a concert, said 'You've got a great gift there, lad. You've got fine breath control, your hearing must be incredibly acute, and you've a wonderful memory.'

That is how I came to make a living – at first a very modest and precarious living – from imitating before audiences at concerts, in music halls, and finally on radio and television, the calls and songs of birds and others of God's creatures.

When I was twenty-one I was laid off from my job as a plough maker in an engineering firm in Ipswich, and in 1929 I got my first engagement as an imitator of birds with the BBC at Savoy Hill. The first person to congratulate me after my performance was an announcer, Stuart Hibberd. I returned to making ploughs in Ipswich during the 1939-45 War, but 'gave in my notice' when the war was over. Since then I have whistled my way to a certain amount of national fame and have made friends with such wonderful fellow 'entertainers' (that is the word I use to describe myself) as Max Miller, Charlie Chester, Ted Ray, Peter Sellers, Cyril Fletcher, Donald Sinden and Morecambe & Wise. Meanwhile, wearing my other hat – as they say nowadays – I have shared happy hours with such ornithologists as the late James Fisher and that fine artist Fish-hawk, Tony Soper, Johnny Morris and David Attenborough.

I am constantly asked by film and radio and television producers to imitate horses, dogs, cats, ducks, turkeys, reindeer (in the *Santa Claus* film), and even mechanical sounds like kettles, sewing machines and bicycle pumps. These present no problem to me at all. The real challenge comes from birds, such as the Nightingale, the Blackcap and Wood Warblers. A Nightingale, for instance, has a huge range of phrases. I practise bird songs every day of my life. I still close my eyes for a few moments every day to sharpen my hearing.

I use my palate. I use the inside of my left or right cheek and by controlling the puffs of air I guide the sounds. I use my stomach and my nose to reproduce certain sounds. Fortunately I have one blessing. None of these efforts affects my throat. I never suffer from a sore throat – perhaps because I do not smoke. I never make any more movement of my face when producing an unusual sound than I do when talking. And I never use my fingers to imitate any bird's voice.

If I hear a harsh cry from, say, a Partridge or a Raven, my cheek muscles immediately tighten. For me, every bird sound I hear has a significance, a rising or falling tone, or some indication of the bird's emotions or intentions.

The real problem is one of memory. There are over eight thousand six hundred species of wild birds in the world. I believe I can imitate the songs of about six hundred of them – so I have quite a way to go yet! I have found that the most effective way of memorizing a bird's song or call is to put it into a phrase of words. If I am asked to imitate the song of a

Redstart my memory prompts me with the phrase 'Why don't you try to follow the rippling river', which is how my ears first recorded it.

This is not an original idea. How else did those who first named the wild birds set about the task? For instance, the names of the Cuckoo, the Chiffchaff, the Coot, the Twite, and many others derive from the characteristic utterances of these birds. This practice is common all over the world. In Africa there is a water-loving bird, an Ibis, which is known as a Hadada, because its call is a loud '*Ah hadada*'. In the United States there are many wild birds whose names have been developed from their calls and song: for example, the Chickadee or the Towee. To prompt my memory and help with my ability of mimicking birds' voices I have merely taken this method a step further.

If you listen to the call of the Little Owl you will find it sounds much like the word 'Will', and if you repeat slowly the call of the Heron it will sound almost like its name. These are fairly simple and obvious resemblances. But the songs and calls of many birds consist of a sequence of sounds, and I try to memorize these with a sequence of words that echoes or expresses that sequence. A wild bird familiar in Britain, whose song is one of the delights of garden and countryside, and lasts almost all the year round, is the Hedge Accentor or Dunnock, who is so often mistakenly referred to as the Hedge Sparrow. As a memory phrase for this bird I have stored in my mind the words 'What did you see? What did you say? What did you do?' Repeated often, perhaps in a whisper, this echoes the bird's regular call.

Anyone with a good ear will find it a fascinating hobby to make his or her own interpretations. Mine for the Mistle Thrush, as you see in my comment in this book, is '*Bye-bye-Dorothy-Dorothy-behave*'. Not all birds whistle, of course, but I have included in this book some Doves, for their utterances can certainly be captured in a memory phrase.

I am often asked if I learn the voices of wild birds from tapes. The answer is emphatically No. I have to try and describe a bird and its actions when I give a talk, and this I can only do if I have discovered from actual observation whether the sound I hear is the bird's full song, or a mating call, or an alarm signal. When I began to broadcast in 1929 my programmes included imitations of such birds as the Chaffinch, the Thrush, the Blackbird, the Robin, the Blackcap, the Chiffchaff and the Willow Warbler. I could not have used a tape then, for tapes were not available. Nor were gramophone records. Not for a moment do I decry the use of tapes nowadays by those who merely want to identify the birds they listen to, but I advise those who do, to find out from visual observation what the bird looks like, and what is the particular reason or occasion for the sounds it is uttering.

It is not just the mechanics of mimicking and decoying birds that interests me. I live my life amongst them, and I never tire of listening to them, watching their different characteristics, mannerisms and behaviour, their habits of courtship, and their methods of nest-building. In my early days I would often sleep out on the heath or by the estuaries of the Deben and Orwell. And today my wife and I visit bird sanctuaries all over England, Wales and Scotland, especially that at Minsmere in Suffolk. But there is no pleasure so great as entertaining birds in one's own garden.

Eighteen years ago, when our family had grown up and moved on, we found our previous house much too large, and we bought a bungalow in an acre of ground on the outskirts of a village in the very centre of Suffolk. It suited us well, and saved us a lot of housework. But there was a snag. It was built on an acre of cold, heavy soil, totally uncultivated, but riddled with the roots not only of buttercups and the lesser celandine but nettles, docks and dandelions. What was worse, there were no trees, no bushes, no birds. Not even a Sparrow.

I tried to encourage birds to come by erecting some poles which I got from the local thatcher, and fixing nest boxes to them. At first there were no takers. But in the second year we found that Tree Sparrows were fighting over the nest-boxes with House Sparrows.

Meanwhile I bought trees, I cadged trees, and I 'liberated' birch trees from the heathlands near by. Soon the garden began to look like a small forest. Then I began to make provision for waterbirds. I dug a ditch that ran the whole length of the garden, and I dug a pond which today looks like a work of nature if one doesn't look too closely at the black polythene at the edges. This pond is now overhung with two tall willows. A mallard was the first resident in the pond, and she brought up a family of ten enchanting little ducklings.

We now have tall Lombardy poplars, hazel bushes, Scots pines, oaks, sycamores, a huge weeping ash, and in fact over fifty different species of trees and shrubs are thriving in this transformed acre of wasteland. I no longer have to roam the lanes as I did as a young man, for anyone who reads the following pages of this book will realize what a vast variety of wild birds visit us in our own garden, and nest there not only in the thirty nest-boxes I have provided for them but in trees and bushes especially chosen and planted to cater for their needs.

Rabbits play at the end of the garden. Hedgehogs are very welcome as they keep in check snails and slugs and grubs. Once a stoat came and stayed for a while. A Heron occasionally visits our pond. We have the long-tailed and the yellow-necked field mice, short-tailed voles, and three kinds of shrews, including a water shrew which astonished my wife when she first saw it diving and swimming in the pond.

INTRODUCTION

Apart from the more common garden birds which you will find described in this book we have Waxwings during the winter – lovely visitors from Scandinavia who feed on the pyracantha berries, also Redwings and Fieldfares and Snipe, which drive their long beaks into the cold wet ground and feast on the worms. And there on the window ledge of the kitchen are the field glasses that can bring any of these creatures close before one's eyes.

It is a cliché that the way to a man's heart is through his stomach, and this is certainly true of birds. When we were faced with a bare garden our only hope of attracting some birds was to offer them a meal. I had an old friend, John Haith, of Cleethorpes, in Humberside, whose business it is to supply food for wild birds. He is known throughout Europe as an expert in providing a variety of different types of food required by wild birds. Our first order was for a hundredweight of peanuts, for there is no food more welcome or nourishing for all sorts of birds. We also ordered the same quantity of his special food for birds which are known as soft-billed. Within a day or two of our placing this in bird trays we were amazed at the assembly of Chaffinches, Goldfinches, Bullfinches and Linnets, and a host of the more common garden birds such as Robins, Blackbirds and Starlings.

Kind-hearted bird-lovers who put out food for their birds are often concerned because of the greed of the larger birds. Such natural bullies as Greenfinches and Great Tits prevent the smaller birds from getting a fair share. (Are not human beings rather like this too?) My wife and I have overcome this problem for we see that the food we put out in the way of household scraps, vegetables and fruit is cut up into small pieces, so that the larger birds have to work as hard as the smaller birds.

Over the years we have learnt to offer variety, for birds are likely to be as bored as human beings if their diet is too monotonous.

We hang up boiled potatoes, each placed in one of those mesh containers in which the greengrocer supplies apples and oranges. If you hang them up in the right place the birds will cling to them as readily as they do to the mesh stockings containing peanuts.

We have also found that all kinds of fat left over from cooking, rendered down, and put in empty milk or cream containers will be much appreciated, and will do the birds a lot of good. Include a few currants and raisins in it, and they will quickly disappear. Stale cake, soaked in sweetened water, is also welcomed, as are any bones left over from a meal. The smaller birds will attack these vigorously to extract any bits of fat or meat left on them.

Meal worms can be bought from various shops specializing in bird food, and are an excellent source of food for most wild birds. But it is wise not to offer too many at a time as they may have the effect of causing loose droppings, and weakening the birds. On the other hand, stale bread (not white) soaked in water or milk to which a drop or two of cod-liver oil has been added, is a splendid tonic both for the adult birds and for the young, especially those fed from the crops of their parents.

If you have room to grow various kinds of wild grass, hang up sprays of them, when ripe, as they are excellent for birds feeding their young, especially Greenfinches. Reed grass carries sprays of fat seeds. When elderberries are ripe we gather them in the hedgerows and hang them up in different parts of the garden.

All kinds of fruit that we use in the house appear to be suitable for wild birds. At one time we had a glut of tomatoes, and when sweetened with sugar these were an instant success. Grapes and small pieces of banana also go down well, and surplus ripe apples if chopped into small sections. The most appreciated of all, as far as we have observed, are the fat seeds of sunflowers, if you grow them as we do, mostly so that we can watch the antics of Titmice as they pick out the seeds.

As I said earlier, in planting and developing our relatively small garden we had very much in mind the bird population that we hoped to attract to what had been an empty space with virtually no trees or vegetation in it. For the benefit of others who want to do the same thing I append a short list of shrubs which are of particular value to birds, either for food or shelter or providing sites for nests. In planting them, however, take care not to crowd them, as they will almost all ultimately fill a lot more space than you might suppose at planting time.

Berberis mahonia aquifolium. Blue berries for most hungry birds.

Buxus sempervirens. Box. Slow-growing, but ideal for nesting and cover.

Carpinus betulus. Hornbeam. Catkins much appreciated.

Ceanothus americanus. White flowers in May and June.

Crataegus monogyna. Hawthorn. Catkins very attractive to birds.

Cotoneaster rotundifolius. Red berries, much appreciated by the red-tailed humble bee as well as by Finches.

Deutzia gracilis. White blossoms in June. Ideal for nests.

Hedera helix. Ivy. Ideal for small nesting birds. Cover in all seasons, and fruit in winter.

Ilex aquifolium. Holly. Abundant red berries for winter. A last resort for Thrushes.

Juniperus. Useful for nests and shelter.

Ligustrum vulgare. Privet. Ideal for nesting and late food.

Philadelphus coronarius. Mock orange, scented. Shelter for nesting.

Prunus serotinus. Black plum or red cherry. Liked by Thrushes.

Prunus virginiana. Choke cherry. Thrush family.

Rosa multiflora. Wild rose. Ideal for shelter.

Rubus fruiticosus. Bramble. Ideal for all wild song birds.

Sambucus nigra. Elderberry. Attracts flies, which in turn attract birds.

Symphoricarpus albus. Snowberry. Beloved by Blackcaps, Garden Warblers and Thrushes.

Viburnum opulus. Guelder rose. Berries for all small birds.

Viburnum opulus florplena. Red berries for all birds.

This book is obviously written for people who have an affection for birds, and regard them as delightful friends. There are some people, however, especially gamekeepers and farmers, who are quick to point out the damage some birds do to their vested interests. They point to those so-called rogues of the countryside, the Magpie and the Jay and the Crow, who intrude into areas which men regard, in every sense, as their preserve. Admittedly, these marauders are to some extent a menace to game such as Pheasants and Partridges, which men are deliberately preserving for their own sport. But even these miscreants have their place in nature, and are responsible for keeping a check on rats, mice, weasels, and vermin of all kinds.

In the fruit season undoubtedly some of the smaller birds 'help themselves' from the trees. Bullfinches especially have got themselves a bad name. But such thieving occurs only in a few weeks of the year, and the damage done is infinitesimal compared to the vast benefits conferred on agriculture by the constant warfare waged by most small birds on aphides, caterpillars, grubs and pests of all kinds.

People who condemn Bullfinches for the damage they are accused of doing to fruit blossom should consider what some other members of the animal kingdom do. The grey squirrel, for instance, wilfully attacks the heads of the horse-chestnut tree, from which lovely clusters of blossom arise. I have seen the drive of a great house near where I live strewn with chestnut crowns. And I cannot understand why, for there seems no reason for their destruction. They are just nipped off by the squirrels and dropped to the ground.

What would happen, I wonder, if by some dreadful accident we were deprived of the services of our wild birds? No concoction created in a chemist's laboratory could compensate for any such loss. One can imagine the savage increase in the massed ranks of aphides, to say nothing of the crawling armies of caterpillars, and the hosts of insects whose ravages would decimate vegetation.

Birds make an invaluable contribution to the balance of nature; and the three hundred thousand or so members of the Royal Society for the Protection of Birds are a noble army whose activities deserve every support.

It is to such people, and those who share their delight in the companionship of birds, that this book is addressed. As will be obvious from the title the emphasis of the book is on those birds who are singers or whose calls are likely to be heard and recognized in gardens, on country holidays and in walks down country lanes, in woods, or across fields, commons and heathlands. Amongst the forty-eight birds

illustrated and described there are a few which are by no means common, and we have had to restrict the choice by omitting birds of prey and birds which frequent the sea and coast, as well as a few singers such as the Hawfinch or the Ring Ouzel, whose songs are by no means negligible, but are rarely encountered.

The choice of birds for the book has been made in close co-operation between myself and Raymond Watson, who is, in my opinion, the most talented bird artist working in Britain today. I feel privileged to have been able to work with an artist who is so accomplished and yet so modest. His accuracy and attention to detail not only of each bird's posture and plumage but also of its background and environment, is almost incredible. One of the delights of my somewhat unusual career is to have been given the opportunity to meet and make friends with Raymond and his wife Peggy, who are neighbours of mine in Suffolk.

I would also like to pay tribute to the publisher's Editor, John Hadfield, another Suffolk man, who originally suggested the idea of this book to me, introduced me to Raymond Watson, and has designed, edited and 'produced' the book so handsomely.

PERCY EDWARDS

O BIRDS, my brothers, sing to me once more
E'er I return again to whence I came,
Give me your joy, your innocence, your lore,
Your air-borne, wind-blown ecstasy I claim
Because ye truly are my brothers dear,
Sing to me once again before I go from here. . . .
The joyful song that welcomes in the spring,
The tender mating song so bravely shy,
The song that builds the nest, the merry ring
When the long wait is ended and ye bring
The young birds out and teach them how to fly:
Sing to me of the beechnuts on the ground,
And of the first wild flight at early dawn,
And of the store of berries someone found
And hid away until ye gathered round
And ate them while he shrieked upon the lawn:
Sing of the swinging nest upon the tree,
And of your mates who call and hide away,
And of the sun that shines exceedingly,
And of the leaves that dance, and all the glee
And rapture that begins at break of day . . .

JAMES STEPHENS
The Hill of Vision, 1912
(By permission of the Society of Authors)

The Hedge Accentor

Prunella modularis

I do not like to hear this small brown bird referred to as a Hedge Sparrow. It most certainly is not a Sparrow, but an Accentor, one of two species known in Europe, the Alpine and the Hedge. Accentor is also an appropriate name if one bears in mind that in the musical world the word denotes the singer who takes the lead in a chorus. This is exactly what this little bird does. It is the first voice to greet, however half-heartedly, the first grey streaks of a new day. Times without number, when walking, as I often did when I was a boy from eight in the evening until eight in the morning, I would hear this shrill voice piping its song. Then there would be silence, followed by the more familiar voices of the Thrush and the Skylark.

This bird has many local names, which is not surprising, for it is well known, and it is resident with us the whole of the year. 'Shuffle-Wing' is one name, for the bird has the habit of flicking its wings over its back when excited, especially when chasing a rival or courting a female; this is something one can see at any season of the year. 'Hedge-Betty' is another name; 'Dunnock' is another, widely used in East Anglia, and 'Blue-Tom', a reference to the head and the neck, which have a greyish blue look.

From January to August the shrill little song can be heard, though from notes I have kept over the years there is very little song after the first week in the latter month. But after a silence of about three weeks it will be resumed, and then will continue right through the autumn and the winter.

The song is a bright collection of notes which lasts barely four seconds. A memory phrase which may help the reader who does not know the song, and one I have used since I was a young man, is '*What - did - you - see, what - did - you - say, what - did - you - do - oo*'. If this is whispered it will convey a good imitation. Treated phonetically it sounds like '*Wee - chee - chee - ur, wee - chee - ay, wee - chee - dee - dee - oo*'.

The alarm note is a sharp '*Spiv*', which can be repeated time and again until the listener is concerned and searches for the reason. Often a Kestrel overhead is the cause, or a cat crossing the garden. Other Hedge Accentors take up the call until the garden rings with complaints. Normally, however, it is a silent little bird.

The nest will be built in any situation which provides good cover, and is skilfully hidden. We have three nests in the garden at the time of writing; one in an ivy and rambler rose which cover one of the fences, another deep within a clump of bamboo by a big pond, and a third in a bramble thicket which is a barrier between the field and a corner of the wild part of our garden. I am fairly sure that there must be another, but one which so far I cannot find. The male bird attacks any Robin or other Hedge Accentor who ventures near a corner where a Canadian redwood raises its pointed head skywards; but its nest is not in that tree but somewhere near.

The nest is a very neat cup of grasses and moss, with twigs at the base and bits of wool which the birds pick up at odd times as if they liked the idea of a little colour. The eggs are very lovely, as blue as a cloudless June sky.

The young when first hatched are ready to open their orange-coloured mouths at the first shadow overhead until caution teaches them that all shadows are not parents bearing food.

This small bird does nothing but good for the garden. The spring and summer diet consists of insects, and these are fed to the young. In the late autumn and winter seeds of various kinds are eaten. This winter diet has prompted me to name this bird 'the poor relation'; for when food is scarce the hedges are crammed with birds of all kinds who are untidy feeders and drop as much as they consume. Down below, like Lazarus gleaning the crumbs, is what I as a Suffolk man call the 'little owd Dunnock'.

16

RAYMOND WATSON

The Blackbird

Turdus merula

> *The Nightingale has a lyre of gold,*
> *The Lark's is a clarion call,*
> *The Blackbird plays but a boxwood flute*
> *But I love him best of all.*

W. E. Henley summed up exactly the mellow flute-like phrases of our yellow-billed neighbour. Not for this bird the polished perfection of others; his voice is an untrained contralto. It is a careless, happy voice; from the orange beak floods a melody that is born of no teacher, no conductor, just a solo whistled in the quiet hour of the twilight. When the red of the departing sun freckles the West he perches against the sky, a dark silhouette intent upon whatever melody comes to mind. Then, with what often seems like a chuckle of sheer joy, he closes his wings and drops like a stone, to run with up-lifted tail through the garden to chase others of his kind.

It is then that the so-called alarm notes ring out, for I have to admit that this lovely bird is a gentle fraud. The Blackbird often behaves like the boy who cried 'Wolf'. Times without number I have gone out into the garden to chase away a cat which I imagined was bothering the bird, only to find that old 'Golden-bill' was merely reminding a neighbour that this garden was his hunting ground. The shrieking notes which sound like '*Twink – twink – twink – twink – twink*' are the same notes that are used when an owl or cat is near. Again they are used just before daybreak, with the same warning to others who are interested in the supply of food, especially of worms. The comical part is that while he chases away a rival, another is already trying to take over, and the Blackbird is the loser in the end.

For all that the lovely song sounds mellow and measured, it is a careless solo from a bird which sings as if each phrase is an after-thought. I have often put the song or at least a particular phrase into words, for example:

'*Call me early in the morning*'. If you think of a deep whistled phrase with that sentence you will have a very good idea of one of the many songs. Another which comes to mind is: '*Well, I declare*', a rich warble. Another which I hear daily is: '*Wait, you're really daft*'.

In addition to the songs, there are many different alarms; the one mentioned above, and then the soft anxious '*Pup – pup – pup*'; this is used a great deal when the young are hidden and the female calls to them for caution. Another is a very thin, almost weeping note, similar to that of the Robin, but shorter and louder; '*Seeee*'. This is used at a time when both hunger for food and alarm trouble the bird. When a rambler comes into view along a lane or quiet road the Blackbird which was quietly singing is shocked into uttering '*Poy – ee – ee – terrerer – twit – twit – twit – twit – twit*'. The flight note is a soft '*Pree – ee*'.

As for domestic arrangements, one must admire the energy of these birds, both the male and the female. No sooner have they with some impatience taught their first brood how to fend for themselves than another clutch of greenish-brown eggs is in the old nest, or in another built on top of the first one.

The nest is similar to that of the Song Thrush, without the dung or mud lining. It seems that the female, who incidentally does all the building herself, has ideas just where the mud or dung should go; she lines her home with it, but she then covers it with soft grasses. A kind of one-upmanship on the Thrush. The site chosen is often in a bush or small tree; sometimes it is high up, and at others it is possible for a passer-by to look into the cup. I have had a Blackbird who built her nest in a nesting-box which was placed in a shrub for the attentions of a Great Tit. Scorning that nest-box the Great Tit had enlarged the hole in another, which I had made for Blue Tits. However well intentioned one is, a bird has the last word in the choice of her home. But a Blackbird in a nest-box, that was really something!

RAYMOND WATSON

The Blackcap

Sylvia atricapilla

I don't know what inspired the legend of Pan, the Greek god of flocks and shepherds, but whenever I hear the Blackcap piping away in the shelter of our birch grove I think of Pan. The connection is rather loose, because Pan is said to have inspired fear. Not so the Blackcap. But when I hear his hesitant opening notes, I think of that odd creature running his bearded lips over his seven pipes before bounding through the woods, piping his carefree melody. The bird sings just such a bright melody, with a bounding, piping lilt.

During the late days of March, provided the winter has been mild, I find myself saying to my wife: 'The Blackcap is singing in the garden'. 'Oh that's good', she says, 'winter is on the way out'. By the middle of April the lively piping phrase rings out all over the garden. I join in, and then the bird and I have a battle of songs. Needless to say I only sing *his* song. The Blackcap is one of the easiest of wild birds to decoy. I have been able to call the bird as many as sixty times into the trees above me, and I was the first to tire, for my tongue was aching. But the Blackcap went on in seeming triumph. It did me the honour of recognizing my imitations as the real thing.

The call notes are a dry '*Sak – sak*', used often when the bird is unable to decide the intentions of the intruder. If I do join in, these notes are a sign of anger that it is not able to locate his rival. Another note, which I only hear when the birds are nesting, is a series of deep notes that do not sound as if the bird made them. This, I am sure, denotes anger, for the restless bird flits about and even shows itself, its head on one side seeking the intruder. The first notes, which I have described as '*Sak – sak*', can easily be imitated by making a kind of human '*Tutting*' sound. This will decoy many small birds: I use it for the purpose of decoying Wheatears, Stonechats, Redstarts and others. It seems that birds have an insatiable bump of curiosity; they just must seek that other bird and drive it away. The song can be identified with ease if the reader will take careful note of the treatment of the sounds which I write down. Remember to whisper them to yourself, and with a little practice you will have the song of the Blackcap.

The timing is important, if you bear in mind that it is a bright pipe and will be hurried along, and finish with an abruptness that seems as if the bird had been interrupted. '*Sit – ip whey – dow sin – tin ter – dadow why – did pee – dee pee – dee*': this last note is often hard and emphasizes the idea of the abruptness. I have timed the burst again and again; sometimes it will fall short as if the bird paused to listen to other sounds, but when in full flow it will last five seconds.

The nest, unlike that of the Willow Warbler, is placed in bushes or shrubs. One shrub which we have is the snowberry, *Symphoricarpus*; not only does the Blackcap choose this as a nesting site but it is very partial to the fruit. I often hear that dry '*Sak – sak*' coming from the depths of this shrub when I go down the garden. I take it as a warning that the Blackcap and his mate are at home and do not want to be disturbed. I go the other way.

The nest itself is a slight affair, as if the two birds had decided that enough was enough. I have found nests in hedgerows that were quite substantial, but the nests in our garden are not the usual deep one made by most Warblers. The five or six eggs, coloured like stones, are blotched with brown and fainter slate marks. There is tremendous variation in the colour of the eggs of the Blackcap; in fact, at times white with only faint markings.

The Blackcap should be protected at all times, in spite of the raids it may make into the strawberry beds. The damage it may do is far outweighed by the good it does in making short work of grubs and caterpillars that decimate our tree foliage, especially those which have the cunning to resemble small twigs. We may not see them at once but the Blackcap does.

20

RAYMOND WATSON

The Bullfinch

Pyrrhula pyrrhula

The name has nothing to do with any fancied resemblance to a bull, though some people believe its big head, powerful beak and heavy build are what gave rise to its name. But it has no more to do with a bull than has the bulrush, 'the rush that grows by the pool': the 'poolrush' became 'bulrush'. As far as the Bullfinch is concerned, the name is a corruption of the northern pronunciation of the word 'bud', pronounced in the north as 'bood', hence 'Budfinch', owing to the destructive habits of this bird whose diet is often the buds of shrubs and fruit trees.

As a songster the Bullfinch ranks low, but the beauty of the male bird, with its red breast, black head, and white rump above a black tail, tends to make it a popular visitor. The strange thing is that in spite of its bright colours it is often the 'pipes' of the bird which attract attention first, for, as with the Kingfisher, nature has a way of using those brilliant hues to blend in with the surroundings. I have often been in the garden watching the tit-like antics of the Lesser Redpolls feeding in the birch trees, and then, moving my field glasses in order to follow the Redpolls through the leaves, I have noticed the Bullfinch reaching up to take a bud. Yet I had not seen it until then, in spite of its brilliant red underparts.

The Bullfinch's pipe is a penetrating sound; and though it is soft, it carries a long way. The bird is one of the easiest to decoy, even the female, for she too has a pipe, though by no means as penetrating as that of the male. It is just the one note '*Tue*', repeated again and again when a rival speaks. There is also a song, and some individuals make more of it than others. I have heard a Bullfinch sing a rather pretty little warble when water has been trickling from a broken pipe. Doubtless the sound of trickling water presented a challenge; but the song which is used from early March until June sounds like this: '*Dur – dur – due*'

or '*Due – dur – dur – due*'. The first notes are deep, and the final note lifted higher. There can be a resumption of the song in August. This, I am fairly certain, is due to the birds' making preparations for yet another brood. Although they have two broods through the season, sometimes they will undertake a third.

The young birds, when the parents are seeking food for them, keep up an endless plea, not unlike the pipe of their parents. It goes on well into the twilight hour. Incidentally, the adult birds feed their young on insects and the larvae of destructive plant pests, such as those of moths and butterflies and various flies. The nest is a fine strong structure with rootlets as a base, and this is built up with a weaving of moss and lichens. The eggs are much like those of other finches: greenish-blue with a clouding of brown or red at the larger end. The cock bird is a most attentive husband. I have never seen him brood the eggs, but colleagues of mine have told me that he will often take over the duties of egg-warmer.

In spite of the damage this bird undoubtedly does in some fruit orchards, it is a bird that I would certainly miss. The trees in our own garden look perfectly healthy. I look carefully at the twigs and examine the buds which 'the duzzy owd bud-pricker', to use a countryman's description, is supposed to have ravaged, and I find little sign of the tree bowing before the raids, apart from a bud scale or so lying on the ground. True, these are not currant or gooseberry bushes, and I admit I have seen the ground beside these shrubs littered with green tips of buds. But the resultant harvest, when gathered, was not a disaster.

If we cannot give this elegant, mischievous creature a complete alibi as far as damage to agriculture is concerned at least it compensates with its beauty. Anyone who is inclined to condemn it should take a look at Raymond Watson's painting and consider whether it should be killed, just because of its mischief. There is enough ugliness in the world without our destroying what is so strikingly beautiful.

The Reed Bunting

Emberiza schoeniclus

This very handsome bird visits our garden each spring, and for a week or two dins away at his little song. Not by any stretch of the imagination can the song be called beautiful, but for the earnest way in which the bird offers it, especially across an area of dense reeds, one must admit the dawn chorus would be the poorer without it.

As might be expected, such a striking bird must have attracted many local names, most of them making reference to the black head and white collar, though there is one that refers to the flight call. This name is 'Chink', and the bird's flight call is exactly that. Other local names are 'Coal-head', 'Ringbird' - referring to the white collar, 'Blackbonnet', 'Toad-snatcher', 'Pit-sparrow', and 'Water-sparrow'. Unfortunately we have no evidence that this bird does more than look over our garden, though there is water available, and there are plenty of flies and caterpillars, of which this bird is especially fond, when feeding nestlings. But he never stays.

At the back of Snape Maltings in Suffolk, where the Aldeburgh Festival takes place, there is a long swathe of reeds with which countless music-lovers are familiar as they walk out in the intervals of a concert. There, an hour after dawn, when the audience has gone home, there is a concert of avian music. There is the soft '*Whee - up*' of the Yellow Wagtail, one of our summer visitors, the '*Swit - swit*' of Swallows flashing by, the mutter of Reed Warblers, the noisy stutter of Sedge Warblers, and the tootling alarms of the fussy Redshanks, while passing Terns are grating '*Kee - air*'. Then, as so often happens, there comes a sudden silence. Even the feathery brown heads of the massed reeds seem to stay still for a few breathless moments. But for one bird the silence has no meaning. Perched at the top of a solitary shrub, in full view, the Reed Bunting sings. His effort has none of the polish or variety of the other birds' songs, but he has the moment to himself, and over the ranks of the reed heads comes '*Swin - swin - see - chissit*'.

Also in Suffolk, at Levington Creek, I used to watch the courtship antics of the Reed Bunting. There is now a marina there, and the entrance I used to use is closed, but I still have vivid memories of this handsome bird showing off to the female of his choice. He would grovel, yes *grovel*; how else can I describe his progress in and out of the dusty areas between the patches of rye-grass? He was flat on the ground, his tail spread out like a fan, and his wings stiffly held out, displaying his charms. His back was a rich warm brown, contrasting with the black head and the white collar.

I have been lucky enough to find a number of nests, nearly always led to them by a nervous male bird, scolding me despite his beakful of small caterpillars. How he could produce such a clear note with a full beak was a marvel to me.

A bird sanctuary just outside Ipswich is a meeting place for Reed Buntings, who will vocally mob any intruders. I was being right royally scolded by a male bird on one occasion, so I moved away, keeping an eye on him. He soon dropped down into a clump of nettles and reed-grasses, but he was up again almost at once, so I assumed that he was feeding his mate. I went over to the clump, and out flew the female, leaving me with a perfect view into the snuggest nest I had seen for many a day, a cup of teased-out grass, with a felting of moss and rootlets, a superb job of construction entirely achieved by a beak. There were no eggs in it, but I had seen some before. They are a washed-reddish-stone colour, with dark markings at the larger end, and there are usually five in a clutch.

24

The Chaffinch

Fringilla coelebs

The Chaffinch singing always brings back to my mind those lines of Robert Browning:

While the Chaffinch sings on the orchard bough
In England - now.

From February onwards, after a silence which has lasted from autumn, we can hear that song which, apart from some differences in the abrupt endings, is the one song we can all exactly remember. The Chaffinch will choose any singing post, on which it will lift its head, open its beak wide, and answer the challenge of any other Chaffinch.

The song begins as if the perched bird was not too certain of the opening notes. But after a slight hesitation away he goes at rattling speed. It is a rollicking little phrase, but ends abruptly as if the Chaffinch had forgotten for a split second how it should end. Those endings are fascinating, for they vary considerably. One regular visitor to our garden ends with the flourish of '*Eet - tit - tit - tit - tit - kit - tur - uv - ur - ur - posit - tit - dictionary*'. Others will have the ending which sounds like '*Kiss - me - dear*'.

This charming bird has such a variety of other notes that it almost rivals the Great Tit in its calls. There is for example a call of '*Sit - it - sit - it*'. This is offered usually during the period when the eggs are being hatched, as if the male bird had all the cares in the world. Another, which is very penetrating, is the call which sounds as if the male bird had just recognized the attraction of his neat little wife, for he calls endlessly, '*Sweet - sweet*'.

The '*Pink*' call is not a call confined to any season, for it can be heard at any time throughout the year. It is a call which has been responsible for many local names for the Chaffinch. 'Spinky' is one and another is 'Whit-finch' - undoubtedly a reference to the '*Sweet*' call.

All birds have a flight note, and it is advisable to be able to recognize them as soon as possible, for it is one of the delights of the garden to be able to identify with complete conviction a bird flying overhead. The Chaffinch calls '*Chup*', a soft note, but easily recognized for what it is. Some experts say that the flight note of this bird is '*Chip*'; but it most certainly is not, in my opinion; it is a soft '*Chup*'; any other description would confuse the beginner. For example, a Tree Sparrow while on the wing calls out in an almost metallic '*Tank*', the Bullfinch a soft '*Whib*'. None resembles the '*Chip*'.

The Chaffinch begins to nest in April; and watching her is a lesson in patience. She gathers moss from the grass, fills her beak, and then flies, say, to a Lombardy poplar, where she welds the moss and other materials onto the bole of the tree with slender branches hugging them close. Having watched this for hours, and moved closer, I found it difficult to see which was the nest and which was tree.

In due course I saw five of the sweetest ash-grey, wine-tinged eggs, speckled with dark brown and black, and I feel privileged to have been able to watch the building and completion of their home. During the months following the end of the nesting period, towards the end of June, only one brood will be reared.

It is a joy watching these trim little birds going to and from their nest with food, and they are still more engaging when the young leave the nest and the parents move across the lawn finding weeds and insects for them, their heads moving backwards and forwards as though they were tiny colourful pigeons. The female is not as handsome as her mate, but she has a certain neatness and pattern of plumage that stamp her as a Chaffinch. The white wing bars show clearly when she flies.

I once heard a Chaffinch singing as I crossed Piccadilly Circus in London. There, in a cage on the edge of an office window, I saw a Chaffinch. Risking my life in the traffic, I stopped and stared. Apparently I was the only person in the crowded street who could hear that small voice.

The Chiffchaff

Phylloscopus collybita

The Cuckoo is so often associated with spring that it has become accepted by many people as the herald of spring. The earliest record I have of the Cuckoo arriving is April the seventh. Yet there is a very small bird, who scarcely measures four and a quarter inches from beak tip to tail tip, which is in my opinion the true herald of this season. I have heard it singing on the twelfth of March.

It is the Chiffchaff; it comes each year some time before most of the trees are showing signs of bursting buds; its journey, when you come to think about it, is a staggering achievement, for the shores of the Mediterranean are its winter home and it must have covered the full extent of Europe on its way.

It is a close relation of the Willow Warbler and the Wood Warbler, and it announces its arrival with a song from which it has been named, '*Chiffchaff*'. It has many local names, but not all are born of its song, for one is 'Dark-footed Pettychaps'; but 'Choice and Cheap' and 'Chip-chap' refer to the double notes which make up the song. I have read comments on the song which I cannot agree with. One described the song as monotonous; another that it has no more attraction than the sound of someone clipping a hedge with garden shears. Anyone who can dub this bright little song, telling of the passing of winter, as monotonous must lack a 'listening ear'.

It sings with us from March until early July, and never did I hear it begin with the phrase 'Chiffchaff'. If one listens carefully the song is '*Chaff – chaff – chaff – chiff – chiff – chaff – chaff – chaff – chaff – chaff – chaff – chaff*', and so on. In spite of that repetition I never find it boring. No. There is a rise and fall throughout the repetition that has a lilt all of its own. Indeed, it seems that the small bird is only too aware of its limitations vocally, and tries to give its song as much variety of expression as possible.

I remember a Chiffchaff singing in Lady-wood, at Nacton in Suffolk, where the BBC were doing a programme called 'International Bird-Song'. Brian Johnston and I were there to decide where microphones were to be erected, in order to catch the full volume as well as the different bird voices. We were standing by one of the lakes when a Chiffchaff began to sing. To my amazement the song was '*Chaff – chidder – chaff – chaff – chaff – chidder – chaff – chaff – chaff – chidder – chaff – chaff*', with a rhyme all its own. I tried the normal song, much to the amusement of the assembled engineers, but the only reply was '*Chaff – chidder – chaff – chaff*', as before. I can only suppose that the bird had what we would call a stammer. Other calls are so soft and gentle that it is difficult to locate the bird. One in particular, because of its tone, must be a distress call: '*Say – die, say – die*'. Another which I have to listen to most carefully is so like a call note of the Willow Warbler that I have often identified it incorrectly. It is a gentle '*Too – ee?*,' as if it questioned the intruder.

Often when the Chiffchaff is in full flow with its song it is possible to hear what appears to be an echo of what has gone before. It seems that the bird is going over the completed phrase, and correcting it before trying the song again.

There is a resumption of the song during September, and what a joy it is to hear! The changes in the vegetation may remind us of the approach of the dark days, while this little song, coming from high up in the trees, can only be described as an echo of spring.

The nest is really a work of art. The Chiffchaff builds the same type of igloo as the Willow Warbler, moss-walled and domed; but, unlike that of the Willow Warbler, it is not made on the ground, but just above ground, in brambles or undergrowth in woods or on commons. The eggs are extremely small, and to come upon five or more of them, glossy white, speckled with purple spots, snuggling in that exquisitely constructed nest, it one of the special delights that nature provides.

RAYMOND WATSON

The Collared Dove

Streptopelia decaocto

Our total of wild birds in Britain, both residents and visitors, is not large; so I think that any wild bird which chooses this country should be welcomed. I well remember my excitement at seeing a small green and yellow finch jumping in and out of the furrows in a field near my home in Suffolk. It was a Serin and I had not seen one before, for although it was quite well known on the Continent, it had seldom been seen before in Suffolk.

Another 'first time' as far as I was concerned was my recognition of a Collared Dove, which was unknown as a nesting bird in Britain until 1954. There had been references to it in the press, and bird watchers had been asked to make notes of its appearance. I saw it when I was passing a cottage at Trimley in Suffolk and at first I mistook it for a Barbary Dove, a domesticated dove that one sometimes saw in cages or aviaries. The wings of this bird, however, were somewhat darker.

It was obviously a male bird, for it was displaying in the recognized dove method of courtship, with a deep bow, then an advance on its red legs, followed by another bow. But its voice was quite unlike that of a Barbary Dove. So I took even more notice. What, I wondered, was the object of the courtship display? There appeared to be no other bird in sight. So I moved a little closer; then I saw to my complete astonishment that the object of his display was a bottle of milk on the cottage doorstep. I could hardly believe my eyes. Displaying to a bottle of milk! I wouldn't have believed that any wild creature would make such a mistake.

Since then the Collared Dove has become common in Britain; a lot of people would say it has become too common. I have had many opportunities to study it in our garden, and I am fond of it. I provide plenty of food for it, but I am not too popular with my wife, who becomes weary of the monotonous three notes of its song. Oddly enough, I have the impression that the bird itself gets rather bored with its vocal efforts, for it sounds as if it is saying, '*It's awful. It's awful. It's awful.*' At other times it sounds as though it is saying '*You burst it. You burst it. You burst it.*' It is a song – if you can call it a song – which can be heard throughout the year.

The Collared Dove prefers conifers to any other tree for its nest, though if these are not available it will choose a sycamore. The nest is typical of the dove family: an untidy platform of twigs with only a token effort at home-making. It lays two white eggs, and in Britain there are two or sometimes three broods a year which are reared successfully. The flight note is most unpleasant, for it is almost an idiot-like snigger; there is no other way to describe it. It is a kind of '*Hur – hur – hew – hew – hur*' as the bird flies into the tree.

Anyone who finds this Dove attractive – and apart from the monotony of its song it is an attractive bird – can easily keep it as a regular visitor if it is provided with various items of food such as that provided for domestic chickens. Household scraps, so long as they are free from spices, are accepted with greedy pleasure. The Collared Dove is a swift bird on the wing, for in typical dove flight it cuts through the air with wonderfully assured flight. The swift, jerky movements are made with disregard for wind or weather.

Unpopular though it is with many country people, and, goodness knows, it is no great songster, I regard the Collared Dove as an interesting addition to our garden birds. It is a wonderful piece of nature's craft, a swift-winged bird which walks with the grace of a ballerina, the little red feet moving with twinkling neatness.

As I have mentioned elsewhere, there is a great variety of wild doves in the world, and one wonders which one it was that returned to Noah and his ark. My guess is that it was either a Turtle Dove or a Collared Dove, though it could, perhaps, have been a Carrier Pigeon!

The Stock Dove

Columba oenas

To include the Stock Dove in a book about song birds in the garden may look like packing a book in order to fill the pages. This is not so, for the Stock Dove is indeed a garden bird, and it has a song. It is smaller and darker than a Wood Pigeon. You will find it especially where there are old trees with holes, either in some of the branches or in the main trunk. Indeed the Dutch name for it is *Holenduif*, a reference to its partiality for nesting in holes, be they in trees, or even in the ground, for old rabbit burrows are often taken over by them.

When we lived at Trimley, Stock Doves built a nest in the centre of a mass of witch's broom, a parasitic growth from a big birch tree. This was only a few yards from one of the bedroom windows, so we had as close a view as anyone could wish for. The male dove was in constant voice with his deep crooning sound, from February until August. Then he began again, and was in full voice until October, by which time we assumed that he and his mate had a second brood to rear.

Their courtship always began with a chase round the garden. As usual the female showed indifference to her mate's approaches, but he was a stern wooer, and his deep song was repeated at regular intervals. Many ornithologists describe the voice of the Stock Dove as a monotonous series of '*Coos*'. I must be listening to a different bird, for I love the sounds, which are a continuous series of delightful phrases. They begin so quietly that it is not easy to realize that the dove is in voice; but then it swells louder and louder, with '*Ooh - look - ooh - look - ooh - look*', distinctly uttered with an accent on the 'look', so clear it sounds as if the letter '*l*' is being spoken. Over the years of our experience with the song of this bird we have come to notice that the sounds are in groups of as many as sixteen and more, if we count them from the first quiet opening. It seems to me as if the bird

has just discovered something of interest, and wants all to share in it. Being a shy bird at first it murmurs its wonder to itself in the soft '*ooh - look*'. This grows in volume as the bird is concerned at a lack of interest. Then as if nervous of the attention it may have attracted, the shy creature slowly softens the sounds until they die away in a gentle murmur.

The nest in the witch's broom was used for a number of years, and the pantomime during the courtship period was really entertaining. The male was such a persistent and ardent lover that eventually his mate got the message. From then on we saw little of her except when he brought food in his crop, which she took as if she were a nestling. What a husband!

The young birds make a pleading, whistling sound, and the patient parents bend their heads down, only to be almost savaged as the young pull the mandibles down and push their heads into their parents' wide-open beaks. During the nesting period the crops of all Doves and Pigeons develop a thick curd which eases away when the young call for food. Pigeon fanciers call it 'Pigeon's Milk'.

As with all pigeons and doves, there are very rarely more than two eggs, and with two broods a season this is regarded as more than enough, for farmers do not care for the members of this vast family.

Though the Dove is traditionally cited as an example of perfect love, it can be most spiteful to others. I have watched a Stock Dove attack a young Partridge; but why I did not find out, unless food was the reason. Even in captivity this family of birds will not allow others to share, and to have three in an aviary is asking for one to be subject to endless attacks by the others. The name 'Stock Dove', by the way, is due to an error of identification long ago when it was assumed that this dove was the wild ancestor of the Homing Pigeon. Actually the true ancestor of the Domestic Pigeon is the Rock Dove.

'Blue Rock' is one local name for it; 'Blue Dove' is another. When it is on the wing it certainly tends to look blue.

The Turtle Dove

Streptopelia turtur

There are two hundred and eighty-nine species of Pigeons and Doves nesting wild in the world. In Britain we have only five, and one of these, the Collared Dove, has been added to the British list since 1954, when it first began to nest. It now nests in almost the whole of these islands.

The Turtle Dove is a summer visitor, reaching us about the end of April. It is often described as a bird of copses, woods and commons, but in my experience it most certainly is also a bird of the garden. We hear the deep croon usually about the first week in May, and from then onwards its voice is one of the most common in the garden chorus.

Unfortunately its food consists mostly of vegetation, and consequently it is not too popular with farmers. But I watch it very carefully, for it is a regular bird with us, and in my opinion it has certain usefulness. Not *all* vegetation is needed by the world of agriculture, and the Turtle Dove consumes with relish chickweed and fumitory, as well as that menace of gardens, the red-leg, or, to give it its botanical name, *Polygonum persicaria*. We grow buckwheat and pink purslane especially to attract this Dove. So if our Doves have any sense there is no need for them to raid the fields for food. One other important item, chickweed, as any bird-fancier will tell you, is a superb conditioner for birds; and the Turtle Dove must be well aware of it. So, added to the other seed-producing wild plants, we let the chickweed have its way in certain parts of the garden.

When King Solomon said 'The voice of the turtle is heard in our land' he referred, of course, to the Turtle Dove, and not the amiable reptile. The Turtle Dove delivers a delightful series of croons, which I firmly believe would be a cure for insomnia if it could be played to a sufferer. During noon on a summer day it is the only voice to be heard, and many times I have nodded off while listening to the deep '*Toor – toor – toor – toor – tot – toor*', in groups of threes or twos.

The song pattern varies, depending, I suppose, upon the different moods of the male bird. In addition to those in the group of four, there is also a double: '*Toor – Toor*' and one that carries three: '*Toor – toor – toor*', even a single note at times. On more than one occasion here in the garden a bird has called as many as a group of five, steady and regular as an old clock: a most dreamy sound.

I mentioned this to one or two local ornithologists, and was greeted with lifted eyebrows and doubtful head shakes, as if I had not counted correctly. But I have heard the five-group sounding just after the noon hour has passed, almost as if the hidden bird, which had been the only voice during the heat of noon, decided to upstage the others. During the routine of courtship the male Turtle Dove seems to go into a kind of trance. He croons at a great rate, and though the sounds are just as dreamy as the others, it is constant repetition: one long continuous series of '*Toors*'.

The love display by the male bird has to be watched as well as heard. He approaches the object of his affections with deep bows, and fans the branches with his widespread tail as he does so. The object of his song takes not the slightest outward interest in his performance. She will fly away into another tree and await his approach. Then, as soon as he gets into his 'act', brushing the branch with his tail, she is off again.

There is, however, another sound, and one which I had never heard until I began to decoy the Turtle Dove. It is as jealous about territory as most wild birds are, and this sound comes after the first '*Toor*'. It is a kind of punctuation, I suppose; it sound like a '*Hoo – ac*', not as loud as the croon, but distinctive enough when the bird is overhead.

The nest, built during May, is a platform of twigs and not a very good job of work at that, for though there are only two white eggs it is a wonder to me that they stay in the nest.

RAYMOND WATSON

The Pied Flycatcher

Muscicapa hypoleuca

This plump little black and white bird is one of the liveliest of our summer visitors. In Wales I have watched it by the hour as it sallied out from its perch to take a fly; but unlike our spotted neighbour in Suffolk, I noticed that never once did it return to the post from which it launched itself. The Spotted Flycatcher, on the other hand, usually makes a habit of so doing, unless it spots another fly on its return.

What a fidget the Pied Flycatcher is; it is never still. It flips its tail up and down, and jerks its wings, until the watcher thinks: 'What a bundle of nerves this bird is'. I can only suppose it is impatient for the passing of a fly or some hapless grub in the long grass below, for it seldom misses any that come in view. Its head is moved first upwards to scan the area above; then it puts its head on one side, to watch what stirs below.

On one occasion I was in Burley-in-Wharfedale with two gamekeepers, and we walked the acres of heather together, their interest naturally being for the welfare of the Red Grouse which nested there. When I stopped to answer the song of a Pied Flycatcher they expressed astonishment that that bird was in their area. I assured them that it was so, for the bird sang song after song, and I have to admit that as far as any rivalry between us was concerned, he won 'beaks down'.

What a bright, joyful song it was, with the bird deciding at times to alter the phrase slightly. Whether or not this was to confuse the other bird, me, I do not know, but the rippling phrases rang out clear and sharp. He sang '*Stip – stip – stip – choyet – cheta – choyet*', and then, as a warning to me not to get too complacent, it was '*Stip – stip – stip – eta – ottery – eta – ottery*'. I wish I could describe for you the expressions on the faces of those two keepers. It was not just admiration – oh dear me, no! Looks passed between

them as if they marvelled at a grown man whistling to a wild bird. Then at last the bird decided to fly over and seek his rival. It flew over to where it imagined the rival to be, and there found three men looking up at it. Promptly it flew back towards the tree again. Both keepers looked at me, nodded, but never said a word – just the nods. I needed no more – those nods were praise enough!

The courtship routine which I once watched by a stream in Colwyn Bay in Wales was a rare treat. What a pantomime! I don't know if you have watched the antics of two Robins when they dispute territory claims – the upright stance, the puffed-out chest; well, this was the attitude of the male Pied Flycatcher I watched. He was trying to impress the female of his choice, and she, true to the guile of her sex, pretended complete indifference. He drew himself up until he seemed all chest and legs, quite delightful! The setting was ideal, for the stream chuckled as it ran below the overhanging bushes, which the sunlight broke through, dappling the leaves. These were reflected by the wavelets and then on to the surrounding area, until the ground seemed to be dancing with the water. Brook language and the song of the Pied Flycatcher, they made music together.

The nest was not hard to find, for when I returned to the spot after a week had passed the hen bird was carrying nesting material into a hole in what was once part of an old pollarded tree. I did not see the male bird help at all. He may have done so, but all the time I watched he just sang. There were other notes that I heard constantly; one was a sharp '*Soo – eet*', I think it was a gentle alarm note, not too concerned, but I imagined it to be a warning to the female that I was near. There was a regular call note that sounded like '*Kip*', which wasn't easy to locate, for the water had many voices and it was not possible in the time I was there to be absolutely certain. Indeed there was much going on which I saw but could not hear, for the voices of the water drowned other sounds.

36

RAYMOND WATSON

The Spotted Flycatcher

Muscicapa striata

As I am writing this a small brownish bird keeps on flying to and from a small black nest-box which I had placed above a rambler rose on the post of a fence. My son and brother-in-law had, over the years, presented me with a wonderful collection of well-made nest-boxes, thirty in all. I just did not know what to do with this black box for, as you may have guessed by now, it was one I had made myself. I am not a carpenter; any cabinet-maker would have wept at this travesty of a bird-box. So I had put it up on a post where the rambler roses would hide it as soon as they began to ramble. To my surprise this small brownish bird had taken a great interest in it.

Soon he had been joined by his mate, and I watched them bring a leaf or two to the box. Then they did not appear for three days, and my faith in my handiwork, which had been restored by their appearance, began to vanish. But they came again on the fourth day, bringing much more substantial nesting material. As the days progressed it was obvious that the birds were not only interested in the box; they were going to put down moss, leaves, teased grasses and some hair. My faith in my carpentry was restored.

The box was in full view from the lounge window, and the rambler had some time to go before it could offer shelter. We have a pair of zoom field glasses, and with a turn of a lever the birds seemed to come to within a foot of us. The cock and hen were so alike that we could never tell them apart, except when the hen was on the nest, showing her spotted face over the ledge of the opening. The cock came almost every minute with food for her, and his beak fairly bristled at times with the wings of captured flies.

His voice was so thin that we needed to have the window open to hear him, but he *could* sing. It was a short and thin performance but there was no doubt about the excellence of the phrase that it sang: '*Sip - sipp - sip - seety*' - just that, over and over again.

When I was a boy local ornithologists would tell me that this little brownish-grey bird was mute. One famous ornithologist called it 'a little dumb darling'. It is not dumb. It is most vocal. But you have to take the trouble to listen. The alarm note, which is also used as a contact note, is a sharp '*U - tic - u - tic - u - tic*': but this little bird has more than the song and the call notes. There is, for example, a note of annoyance which is used when an intruder disobeys the call to move on. It begins with the usual '*U - tic*' and then is prolonged into a slurred grating '*Zee - zuuk*'. It is not easy to put that sound into writing, but I have no doubt that it is as near to exasperation as a bird can convey.

Some time later we were able to go out and take a peep at the contents of the nest. The male bird was in constant attention to his mate, and I decided that there must be eggs. There were. The female flew off as soon as we appeared; so we took only one quick look and afterwards we watched from the house. To our immense joy there were five eggs; they were of a rather greenish stone colour, with some red spots well sprinkled over the whole egg. But the larger end carried a sort of halo, something that is often present on wild birds' eggs. I have seen such a halo on the eggs of the Red-backed Shrike and others.

As soon as the eggs were hatched the two parent birds were back and forth all day catching flies. Their energy made us feel guilty about the time we spent watching. They kept up the contact call of '*U - tic*' almost all the while they worked, until we almost believed that they were speaking to each other.

From early daylight to darkness they worked, first on the small Japanese maple, then on the head of a stone statue of Saint Francis; then they moved from the purple sycamore to the cherry, from the silver birch to the horse-chestnut. I guess that never a fly passed without being snapped up. We could hear quite plainly the snap of the beaks.

RAYMOND WATSON

The Goldcrest

Regulus regulus

The Goldcrest is the smallest British wild bird, and, for that matter, the smallest bird in Europe. It has many local names, as can be imagined, for its size alone would attract a number. One I am very fond of is 'Tot – o'er – Seas'; another is 'Tidley Finch'. I have known the bird since my childhood days, but it was only during the past six years that I have been able to call it one of my neighbours. It nested in a Scots pine copse in our garden.

For six years, until the bitter winter of 1984, I used to sing a duet with a Goldcrest, who on his part sought to identify his rival. But as I am not able to create that suspended miracle which is its nest, he seemed to tolerate me, and certainly he taught me how the song of a Goldcrest should sound.

The song seldom varies, making this tiny soloist one of the few garden birds whose voice one can always identify. Try to whisper these notes and you will have it: '*Tee – der – tee – der – tee – der – tee – der – tee – der – dit – it – dit – it – show*'. It lasts barely four or five seconds, but the output of songs in the space of one minute is astonishing. It will sing a few notes, then reach up, showing its orange-red crown, before picking with daintiness an aphis from the base of the pine needles. It wipes its tiny beak sidewards on a pine twig, and resumes the song. I have counted as many as eight songs in one minute.

This outburst of vocal power is at its best during May and June, especially early May, when the female is busy with nesting material. Then the male bird keeps up an outpouring of songs, with short intervals while he sidles up to his mate with items of insect food. These she accepts with the usual wing-quivering, so characteristic of nesting females.

The contact call is a much-used note which often gives a clue to the tiny bird's whereabouts. Otherwise, because of its liking for the higher branches in conifers, it would be overlooked. This note is a hard '*Seeid – seeid – seeid*'. It is a restless bird while calling, and is never still for a second. It searches beneath the base of the pine needles and with not a great deal of success tries to hang upside down in the manner of the Tits.

Once, while resting beneath the Scots pines, I had caught the interest of a male Goldcrest. I was sleepy and was getting a little weary of keeping up the question and answer when he appeared right above where I sat in a deck-chair. I kept my eyes as still as was humanly possible, for nothing scares a wild bird more than a direct look from the eye of a human. Stillness often bothers them, and until the movement of an eye they are often puzzled by it. Well, I began to imitate the song while he reached up to some mite in the pine twigs. Then, to my surprise, he gave what I can only describe as a call of exasperation. It was nothing like any of the normal calls, and most certainly not like the song. It was more like that of a distant Robin, thin and angry. What was most comical was the way in which he reached up to his full height of three inches and a bit in order to give me these notes. I had never heard this sound before from a Goldcrest, and I have never heard it since.

The nest, as with so many nests of wild song birds, is a miracle. How this tiny morsel of flesh and feathers can create such a masterpiece I cannot begin to understand. One day when the parents were both away, feeding and calling in shrill voices to each other, I got the household steps and took a quick peep into their little creation. It was on the pine branch; this alone was unusual, for the nest is usually suspended below a conifer branch. But what a wonder it was, a snug ball of moss crocheted with spiders' webs, a cup of perfect roundness, containing nine, yes, nine tiny eggs, near-white, with reddish spots at the larger end. Did I say the *larger* end? Dear lord, they were so incredibly tiny, those eggs, the wonder was that inside each one there lay curled an even tinier mite, waiting to be hatched out into the miracle of life.

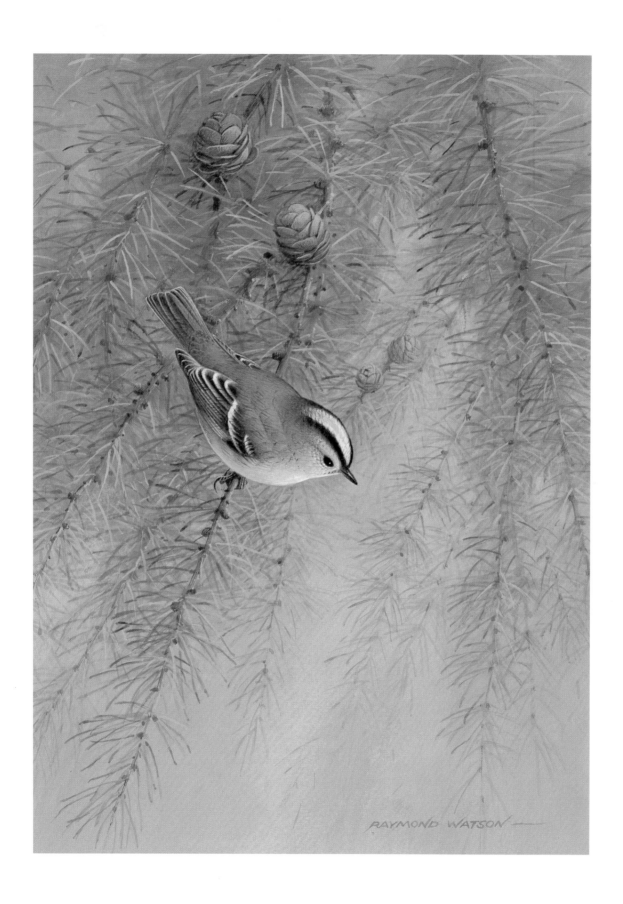

RAYMOND WATSON

The Goldfinch

Carduelis carduelis

When I was a boy this proud and beautiful little bird was in danger of extinction. Thousands were trapped for the cage-bird market. Protection saved it; and none too soon. It became, and still is, an offence to trap it or cage it. And it is now, I am glad to say, quite a common wild bird in the countryside. During the spring and right through to the autumn its liquid notes, especially during flight, can be heard as it crosses over our garden to gather food where there are thistles and other seed-bearing wild flowers.

The Goldfinch has many local names, and many of them reflect its brilliant colours. The local name I like best is 'Proud-Tailor'. Others are 'Seven-coloured Linnet', 'King Harry', and 'Thistle-Finch'.

In our garden we leave thistles to bloom and seed, in expectation of visits from Goldfinches. Their conversation whilst feeding is a delight. And anyone who spares a moment to watch the antics of a Goldfinch selecting a seed from a thistle-head is certain of a reward. The bird picks at the seed-head as carefully as a surgeon wielding his probe. The thistle seed-head is ingeniously fashioned by nature to be carried away on a tiny little parachute which floats in the wind. The Goldfinch does little harm to the massed ranks of packed seeds, but it is a pantomime to watch it selecting a seed and releasing it from the feathery parachute, which then floats away across the garden, accompanied only by a sweet lilting song: '*Sit – ee – swit – ee – swit – ee – swit – ee – purrer. Tot – it – tet – eet – cheeow*'.

The call is a note borrowed from the song. The liquid '*Twit – it – twit – it – twit – it*' is often the only clue that a Goldfinch is passing overhead. There is another note that is almost certainly an anger note. It reminds me of a note used by the caged Budgerigar, a kind of '*Seer*', and is used when Goldfinches are quarrelling. It is a harsh note, with a rasping sound that is not easy to put into words. It should not be confused with the softer note of the Greenfinch. There is also a call which reminds me of one of the calls of a caged Canary, and to my hearing it has a quality of sound almost as if the bird were asking a question; it is '*Whyee – whyee*', a sweet call, yet it has some anxiety about it.

The Goldfinch was the first bird to choose one of our smaller trees for its nest. This was an apple tree so small that we could look over into its branches. The Goldfinch built a small cup of moss and grasses and lined it with the groomings of our Pekinese dog's hairs. These were blond; and the female collected these hairs in her beak until they looked like an enormous moustache.

The nest held five bluish-white eggs that were faintly marked with lines of red. They looked so snug on the lining of dog hairs that I became almost lyrical about them. My wife chided me: 'But they are not *your* eggs'. True, but I felt that somehow I had made the effort to attract them, and I had more than a passing interest in their welfare.

The mother nested for a second time that season, but for some reason she placed this new nest in a tall thin conifer which looked like a pointed green chimney. Alas, the small neat cup that was the nest filled with water each time it rained; so the bird deserted it. Incidentally, she did all that work on her own; her mate just perched above the site and sang his heart out. As far as I could observe he never even helped with gathering material for the nest. Perhaps he disapproved of the place she had chosen. He was right.

As the years pass we look forward to the return visits of this exquisite little bird and the sight of the daintily stepping pair searching our lawns for mosses out of which to construct their snug ball of a nest.

A flock of Goldfinches is collectively known as 'a charm', and this is a marvellously apt and poetic description of them as they pass overhead, their liquid notes floating down.

RAYMOND WATSON

The Greenfinch

Carduelis chloris

Such a superbly tailored bird must have many local names, though one moment of watching the male, resplendent in its spring plumage, persuades me that the name 'Greenfinch' is the best of all names for it. The others do little more than emphasize its green neatness. 'Greenulf' is one; 'Greenbird' is another. So, too, is 'Green Linnet' though this gives rise to the idea that it is a kind of Linnet. It is not. There is yet another name, and this is 'Joey'. This is a local name which I approve, for 'Joey' is a surprisingly exact imitation of the call '*Chodey*'. Variations of this will sometimes sound just like a kitten in distress. Yet another call, which is rather similar to the 'Joey' call, is '*Mary*', '*Mary*', '*Mary*'. Another call note which is very common has a harshness in its whistled sound: '*Zee-Air*' or '*Sea-air*'. This note is offered with the head held high, and is repeated so often that many folk get a little weary of it.

At feeding times the young are led to the feeding table while the parents make the food as soft as possible by working it in their beaks before pushing it into the mouths of the young. They also take the young into the tall grasses where they reach up and pick seed heads which they feed to the fledglings.

The song is often offered while the bird is on the wing, oblivious of everything but the song it is singing. In the song of the Greenfinch there is nothing but happiness. It is not of a high order musically, but the way the brief phrases are sung makes it one of the most cheerful voices of the garden. If you whisper its notes with a sibilant sound you will have '*Chid - did - did - did - Chow - chow - chow*'. This is the complete song but, mixed with the more famous such as those of the Blackbird and Robin, it helps to create a medley that is sheer joy.

The Greenfinch nests in a variety of places in our garden. It will choose the rambler on the fence or the tall Canadian redwood. But they always like to place the nest well up in the site, and if I want to look at the progress of the eggs or the young I have to get out the garden steps. We find the first nests in April, and a second brood is normal. The eggs are bluish-green, spotted and blotched at times by streaks of brown or black, and usually five in number.

In the winter it is one of the birds which readily take the food we put out, a wild bird food with a balanced variety of seeds. It will also feed on brown bread pieces, and a little fruit such as soaked currants or raisins. Indeed all our resident birds relish these extras. But if a Greenfinch is about the other birds will keep their distance. The Greenfinch is a natural bully but only so far as much smaller birds are concerned. I have seen it open its wings wide in a manner calculated to intimidate a small bird on the peanut holders. It will not only open its wings but also its powerful beak, and I imagine that a nip from that is not too pleasant. I must say that the House Sparrow will not tolerate such bullying, for it will give as good as it receives, and often the bully will give way, though it will return again and again to the battle. But the smaller birds, such as the various Tits, have a miserable time when several of the Greenfinches gather, for not only do they lose out with the peanuts but they have to make way for the bullies, who even fight among themselves.

Whatever faults the Greenfinch may have in this direction, its beauty of shape and colour, even the bounding flight, are objects for admiration. It is a lovely bird: Raymond Watson has captured with great skill the superb blending of the feathers and the brilliance of the yellow wings that one doesn't notice except when the bird is in flight. I have often listened to enthusiasts extolling the beauty of birds such as our Kingfisher, Goldfinch and Green Woodpecker, but it is not often that we read of the perfection of the colouring of the male Greenfinch. It ranks alongside those for sheer polished beauty.

44

RAYMOND WATSON

The Sky Lark

Alauda arvensis

The Sky Lark is probably the most easily identifiable of our wild birds when it is on the wing and singing. Few people observing it high in the sky, with its cascade of melody dropping earthwards, are likely to confuse it with any other bird apart from its close relation, the Wood Lark.

There is one note which is used constantly, a sharp '*Pee – irr – irr*'. This is offered at any time, even when in the winter the bird only rises a few feet and gives the idea that it is about to climb higher and higher, but instead drops almost at once. It is also used as a warning note when the nest appears to be threatened.

This is the song I wrote down one fine June morning on a cliff top by the seaside. There was hardly a breath of a breeze. As the bird rose on fluttering wings and reached for the sky this was its song: '*Tirr – ee – er – tee – tee – oo; tir – ee – er – tee – tee – tee – oo – tirr – ee – er – tee – tee – tee – oo, tirr – ee – er – tee – tee – tee – tee – oo – tirr – ee – er – tee – tee – tee – oo – tirr – tee – tee – tee – oo – tirr – tee – tee – tee – tee – oo – tirr – tee – tee – oo – tirr – ee – er – tee – tee – tee – tee – oo – sip – sip – sip – sip – sip – sip – sip – sip – sip – sip – sip – sip – sip – Pee – oo – tirr – pee – ee – tirr – oo – pee – ee – ooo – tirr – Pee – pet – ee – tir – pee – pet – ee – tir – pee – et – ee – tirr – pee – per – pee – per – pee – per – pee – per – pee – per – pee – per, pee – pee – oo – pee – pee – oo – pee – pee – pee – oo – pee – pee – pee – oo – pee – pee – pee – pee – oo. Sit – ee – sit – ee – sit – ee – sit – ee – sit – ee – sit – sit – ee – sit – ee – sit – ee – Chee – chee – chee – chee – chee – chee – chee – chee – chee – chee – chee – chee – cheeoo – chee – ee – chee – oo – chee – chee – chee – chee – oo – chee – chee – chee – chee – oo*'.

The above notes faithfully record the song if they are whispered with a lisping kind of sibilance.

After those '*Chee – chee*' notes the song seems to be no slower, but even more deliberate, as if the soaring bird was supremely confident of its vocal mastery. The tempo changes to '*See – ter – see – ter*', the spaces between each note noticeably slower, until it is possible to follow each note without any difficulty.

I have often timed the song from the first leap until the return to earth again. I have marvelled at the bird's energy; on a never-to-be-forgotten day one bird stayed aloft for seventeen minutes and ten seconds. I had it in full view all the while. No other Lark swung over into the flight path of my bird. On many an occasion I have timed a Lark who sang for over five minutes. And the bird whose song lasted for that record time I had in full view. I watched the swollen throat bulging with the effort of the song, the long wings beating at the air, lifting the bird at each flutter. What a package of energy! The song went on and on, with never a sign of exhaustion, each note clear and sweet, each phrase changed without the slightest effort: an incredible performance.

As it neared the ground on its return flight I expected the bird to drop like a stone. But not a bit of it; it ended the song, fluttered round for a while; then the long wings were arched above its back and the tail held like a rudder, and it made a swooping glide to grassy cover. Small wonder that poets down the ages have immortalized it. Shelley wrote his famous poem 'To a Sky Lark'; Wordsworth called it 'the pilgrim of the sky'. Meredith captured it in one superb sentence: 'He drops a silver chain of sound of many links without a break'.

The Sky Lark never nests anywhere but on the ground, perhaps in a hollow where a horse or a cow has dug a deep print. Using this as a base the bird lines it with dry curled grass; three eggs or at times five, of a mottled brown, match the surroundings perfectly. The Sky Lark will use the same nest again once the young have learned to find for themselves, when yet another clutch is laid.

RAYMOND WATSON

The Wood Lark

Lullula arborea

The Wood Lark is without doubt one of the sweetest singers of native wild birds. Time and again I have stood and listened as the bird let fall to earth those lovely liquid phrases. Even when perched on a twig it seems to be imbued with the same carefree happiness. Down by the shores of the Orwell I used regularly to hear it singing. As I walked down the winding path which led to the river I seemed to hear it above all other voices.

Sometimes in the cool evening air a mistiness would appear between my field glasses and my eyes, and I had to wipe my eyes with a handkerchief lest I missed the sweeping circles in which the Wood Lark flew. I venture to mention this embarrassing recollection of Percy Edwards being overcome by emotion, because an earlier, far more important and famous naturalist than I, Gilbert White of Selborne, was affected in much the same way whilst listening to the same bird. In 1788 he wrote:

> *Blended objects fail the swimming sight,*
> *And all the fading landscape sinks in night,*
> *While high in air and poised upon its wings,*
> *Unseen, th'enamoured Woodlark sings.*

An unsentimental eyebrow may be lifted at the mention of this bird singing at night, but, as I know from experience, this is often a regular occasion, especially if the night is warm and windless, and if the nest-building is completed. Then it takes little to tempt this lively bird into the sky, from whence songs fall earthwards like handfuls of silver.

The song is also a wonderful addition to the dawn chorus. Whilst other voices rise from spinney and lane, the song of the Wood Lark, coming from high above, seems almost like a teacher leading a choir. The bird flies round and round in ever-widening circles as it climbs. At times, when the wind is rough, the Sky Lark will swing round in a circle as it battles with gravity, but in the flight of the Wood Lark the circles are part and parcel of its display. It will rise to a tremendous height, swinging round and round; and even when returning to earth it still sings with great power. Its song has not the variety of its larger relation, the Sky Lark, but it has a kind of elfin beauty, especially from March to June, though there is always a chance of hearing it again during October, when many of our wild birds recall their spring songs.

I wrote the following notes of its song a long time ago, but I don't think I have to alter them now. One of the most common phrases is '*Tee - oo, lu, lu, lu, lu*'. Another is '*Lill, lill, lill, lill, lill, lill, cher, chee*'. This is followed at once with '*Till - et - Till - et - Till - et - Till - et - Till - et - Chee*', and '*Tee - bet - tee - bet - tee - bet, chee - bet - doy - chee - doy - chee*' and '*Per - chay - Per - chay - bet - Per - chay - bet - Per - chay - bet!* Then '*Weet - weet - weet - weet - weet - Woy - Woy - Woy - Woy - Woy - Woy*'.

The chief way to distinguish the Wood Lark from the Sky Lark is to look for the much shorter tail when it is flying. The nest is typical of those of the smaller birds that nest on the ground, such as the Sky Lark and the Pipits - a shallow saucer, walled with grass, supported by moss, and lined with any local materials such as teased-out grasses and, if possible, some hair. The eggs are usually five in number and have a dull white background with a cluster of brown markings.

Sometimes when I was cycling along the lanes on my way to the shores of the Orwell I would come across a Wood Lark singing on the wire from a telegraph pole. Somehow the song never seemed quite the same as when the bird was singing on the wing. When the bird flew from the telegraph wire and began to move in ever-widening circles into the sky above the surrounding trees, its song would become fuller. I formed the impression that the bird needs space and the freedom of the sky to make the most of its song.

48

RAYMOND WATSON

The Linnet

Carduelis cannabina

This is in every respect one of the most attractive visitors to our garden. Its plumage is so well interpreted by Raymond Watson that I would not be so presumptuous as to describe it in words. Its voice, either in song or in call, whether the bird is in flight or perched on a bush, is calculated to make any gardener stop work and look upwards.

In chorus the song is of such high quality that I regard it as one of the most beautiful sounds the countryside has to offer. But there are times when I have been out in the heathland, and the approach to noon has quietened most of the furze-loving birds, and a single Linnet has appeared at the top of a bush of broom and begun to sing its full song as a solo. That is even more miraculous. The phrases are so enchanting that I could have thought I was listening to some creature from another world. If the reader thinks that comment is fanciful he or she has never had the good fortune to listen to a solitary Linnet singing, not for rivalry with other birds or to establish territorial rights, but from the sheer pleasure of opening its throat.

Many times I have tried to write down the full song in words, but I have found them lacking in a true memory phrase. I have found the phonetic treatment the most satisfying. The following may give some idea of the full song as a solo from a single bird: '*Chatup - chatup - chatup - tyre - pit - ur - tur - tur - tee - der*'. It can vary, and often does, for individuals will offer delightful surprises. On other occasions they give such an indifferent performance that it seems another species altogether is singing.

Mind you, to be fair, the time of year has a lot to do with it, for the song periods of the Linnet are at their best from April to June, when it will, especially towards evening, give its most delightful performances.

The call notes, which I compare to those of a Redpoll, are less harsh offerings of the '*Cha - cha - cha - cha*' notes: they do not carry the dry tones of the smaller bird. The Linnet has also a most endearing note, and one that I have known from childhood. I believe it is a note of caution, but is so sweet that I have no hesitation in mentioning it in this book, for it is a common enough sound. I have heard it many times when sitting near the nesting site. It is a soft '*Toit*', wonderfully plaintive, and if listened to for a length of time tends to be rather distracting.

The nest of the Linnet is built early in April, but the eggs, which are usually four in number, are rarely laid before the second week. The bluish-white eggs lie at the bottom of a nest lined with thistle-down. We found one in the garden when the BBC visited us to film 'Gardener's World'. It was deep in a clump of bamboo, almost on the ground. The young were by then hatched and as we approached they raised wide-open pink mouths in expectation of a meal. But they closed them immediately our shadows appeared over the bamboo clump. Then the adults appeared in the big willow across the pond and told us in no uncertain manner that their territory was not to be invaded, even by the BBC. The camera team's chief concern, I am glad to say, was for the birds, not the film.

The Linnets nested with us for a second time that year, and successfully reared all five young. We played foster parents to them and tried to help them by putting down close to the site of the nest in the bamboo helpings of the special food I buy for these soft-billed wild birds. It is a mixture of insects, honey and meal. Despite our efforts to make life easy for them we came in for the same scoldings as the BBC camera men were subjected to. I assume the reasoning faculties of a Linnet are not quite as well developed as its gift of song.

Like so many of our wild song birds the Linnet is entirely beneficial to gardens and indeed the countryside generally. Its diet consists of seeds and the grubs of flies, moths and butterflies, such as the Cabbage White.

RAYMOND WATSON

The Nightingale

Luscinia megarhynchos

'The Nightingale, if she should sing by day, when every Goose is cackling, would be thought no better a musician than the Wren.' So wrote Shakespeare in *The Merchant of Venice*. It surprises me that such an observant man should have been unaware that the Nightingale sings far more during the hours of daylight than it does at night. True, the Wren has for its size a most powerful voice, but the Nightingale has a tremendous range which floods the morning as well as night. Even the most famous of the daylight chorus, such as Thrush and Blackbird, are but ghosts of sound when the Master sings. The song is such a marvel not only because of its phrases but also its timing. There is a deliberate build-up to the temendous finale, a superb ripple of notes as if the bird was well aware that the song was coming to a conclusion.

I first heard it when I was fourteen years old; surely, I thought, here was one bird voice that I would never be able to imitate. The range was unbelievable. Since those days I have learnt to produce it from my own throat. I can follow the whole song note by note.

The song begins slowly at first, the notes so thin that there is a kind of ventriloquial effect. It is difficult to be sure just where the hidden bird is. The next notes are abrupt and rather dry-sounding. These are followed by more short notes, but then, from out of what seems to be nowhere, there comes the deep contralto, with the same ventriloquial effect, deep and wonderfully measured. Then, what I consider to be the best of all, come double notes, one deep and the other sharp. They are so deliberate and so slow at first that it seeems the bird's concern is to silence any rival who might have ideas of intruding into occupied territory. The final phrase is rippled away at great speed, and ends with a flourish.

I have written the following notes from the song as I know it. I have also included the so-called '*Jug* – *Jug*' notes, though they sound to my hearing more like '*Dod* – *Dod*'. The opening is '*Sin* – *sin* – *sin* – *sin* – *sin* – *sin* – *sin* – *sin* – *sin* – *per* – *chu* – *chup*'. '*Pit* – *it* – *wit* – *it* – *wit*'. '*Who* – *who* – *who* – *who* – *who* – *who* – *who* – *who* – *Per* – *er* – *er* – *err*'. '*Wot* – *ee* – *wot* – *ee* – *wot* – *ee* – *wot* – *ee* – *wot* – *ee* – *wot* – *ee* – *wot* – *ee*'. These notes are slow, and then they build up into a lovely burst of the so-called '*Jug*' notes, which I have written as '*Dod* – *dod* – *dod* – *dod* – *dod* – *dod* – *dod* – *dod* – *dod*', much quicker than the double notes. There may be odd notes that are quite out of character with what has gone before; but the final phrase makes up for any lapses; these are offered in a ripple of sound as one note follows the other at great speed: '*Pyrr* – *it* – *it* – *it* – *it* – *it* – *it* – *it* – *it* – *it* – *it* – *it* – *it* – *it* – *it* – *it* – *Perrer* – *iding*'. Other notes are the alarm and distress calls and these are either made as a single note or joined together: '*Weet*', and a frog-like '*Corr*' or '*Weet-Coor*'.

After the eggs are hatched there is no more song. The nest is so well hidden it is only possible to find it by watching the adult birds going to and fro; my wife and I have found several, but after the discovery we never visit the site again so as not to leave a track to its whereabouts. The eggs are usually five in number and are a polished olive-brown. The nest is cunningly hidden, usually on the ground or near to it, covered in a mass of leaves.

I have said before how unnecessary it is for me to describe a bird when Raymond Watson's paintings are on the opposite page; but in this case I am going to pass on a description of a Nightingale I watched in company with an old Suffolk gamekeeper. A male bird was spreading his russet tail and dipping his wings, and then, as if deciding that he might be losing some dignity, tightening his feathers. The old man whispered to me: 'Hay look good, don't hay! I will tell you supin, bor. Hay look as if his grub do him a bit o' good'. It was a tribute to a well-built, neatly plumaged bird. 'Bor', by the way, is a Suffolk abbreviation of neighbour; 'hay' means 'he'.

RAYMOND WATSON

The Nuthatch

Sitta europaea

The Nuthatch is not the most striking of wild birds as regards plumage, but from February onwards it is impossible to overlook its strident call of '*Spring - spring - spring*'. And you can watch it defying gravity by climbing the tree bark either upside down or the right way up, or, as an afterthought, dropping tail-first in order to make sure that it does not miss an unfortunate mite hiding in a crevice.

Raymond Watson has painted this neat little bird with his usual skill, so I will not attempt to describe its plumage, except to suggest that it is rather like a Kingfisher that has been too many times to the laundry, with some loss of the Kingfisher's vivid blue and chestnut colours.

I watched a pair clean out a hole in a sycamore tree one spring morning, and the energy of these birds made me feel exhausted, just watching. They brought mud, and with amazing skill began to close up the hole until it was the size they imagined it should be. Nature herself could not have bettered that neat hole. Then to my surprise they kept popping in and out, first one and then the other, until I began to wonder whether or not they were going to nest there after all. So much work had been done; yet here they were apparently trying to make up their minds as to whether or not they were happy with the result. I should have known that no children of nature have time to waste. What they were doing was perfecting the entrance hole and making it smooth; it was a job that a human plasterer would have been proud of.

After this they took what looked like pieces of bark into the hole, but I was sure that leaves were also included as nesting material.

The male was as noisy a bird as I have ever heard. He would lean out from a twig as if defying gravity, and shout - there is no other word for it - notes that sounded just like '*Spring - spring - spring*'. This was not the song, for after a while he began to climb the trees nearby and change to a conversational note which sounded like '*Toit - toit - toit - toit - toit - toit*'. Then he was away with another call, which to my hearing sounded like one of alarm, for, instead of the spring call, it was '*Feer - feer - feer - feer - feer - feer*'. Was there ever a brighter ripple of a voice that spring morning? It carried sheer joy of living, with, I suspect, pride that the home was ready and his mate was sitting. It was a ripple; this is the only way to describe it - a clear ripple of '*Kiv - wiv - wiv - wiv - wiv - wiv - wiv - wiv - wiv - wiv - wiv - wee - ee*', a song full of charm.

Once or twice he was joined by his mate, and they had yet more notes for me to copy. Some were very like thin, high-pitched calls of the Goldcrest, or again like the Tree-creepers, when they get excited - a kind of lisping chatter.

The nesting arrangements I can only guess at, but, as I said, the material I saw taken in was dead leaves and pieces of bark. I know what the eggs look like for the halves of empty ones were brought out and dropped into the plantation where the sycamore trees were. They have a white background and red spots at the larger end. They vary, as do most of the eggs laid by a wild bird, but there was a distinct resemblance to the eggs of the Great Tit; and the colour was the same.

The Nuthatch should have the protection it deserves, for it can do no harm to any garden, and the food with which it feeds the young is flies and caterpillars.

Here is a footnote. Some years ago I received from a listener to my radio programme a box which weighed so much that the postman was curious about its contents. No wonder, for it contained two and a half pounds of dried mud which a pair of Nuthatches had used whilst plastering up a hole in a tree. What energy! These small birds had somehow gathered the mud from heaven knows where. The incredible number of journeys they must have made passes the imagination.

The Tawny Owl

Strix aluco

It may come as a surprise to find an owl included in a book which deals with song birds, but one has only to listen to a Tawny Owl in full song to forget the hour and the superstitions which go with it, for the bird *does* sing.

The hour and the time of the year make so much difference to the reception of that bird and its singing. Hear it on a moonlit night, when the air hangs heavy with the breath of young lilac and the heady tang of hawthorn, then a Tawny Owl's singing seems a delightful performance. But if the month is February, the night is cold, the trees are leafless, there is a heavy mist, and an Owl sings to your lonely ears, it is a haunting sound.

I have decoyed a Tawny Owl on many occasions, even during the bright sunlight of a summer day. It has always answered, but with a peevish reply, resenting being disturbed. After a while, when apparently the unseen rival does not depart, he comes seeking him, and presently it is possible to see the Owl peering short-sightedly through the leaves, with his head bent forward and moving from side to side. I am always intrigued to notice that his throat is the only part of him that moves when he answers, for his beak seems barely to open. I have noticed the same thing with the Wood Pigeon and the Cuckoo. The throat moves as if the bird was swallowing, but the sound is as clear and sharp as it sounds at night. After a while he launches himself and swoops over to where he imagines the sound of his rival came from, but no sound comes from the big broad wings, for all owl wings are soft-pinioned. It would be unwise of nature to have a night bird hunting with noisy wings; rodents' hearing is acute.

The song of the Tawny Owl has often been described as a long hoot, but that description conveys nothing of the make-up and timing of the three phrases which comprise the song. It begins thus; a long-drawn-out, steady '*Ohh –*

ooh – ooh – ooh – ooh – ow'. There is a pause as if the bird was thinking over the first notes, then after about six seconds there comes a short note, then almost at once a long quavering note: '*Ooh – ooh – ooh – ooh – ooh – ooh – ooh – oh – oh*'.

Both male and female take part in a duet, the male with his version of how it should sound, and in reply she gives way to what Shakespeare quoted when he wrote " 'Tu – whit – tu – Whoo' the old brown owl wakes up at night when watch dogs howl", but what he did not know was that it was the female who made that kind of lament. The female calls '*Tu – whit – tu – wit – tu – wit*' getting shriller as it progresses, then '*Tu – wit – tu – weet – ooh – ooh – ooh*', ending on an almost hysterical note, it is so shrill. The young Tawny Owls also call that shrill '*Tu – Wit*' note during July, when they must be conscious of the growing power of their wings. It is then that they offer a much shriller version of the female Tawny Owl's notes. There is also a short '*Kek*' which I believe is a hunger note. One other call which we sometimes hear from the trees opposite is another form of duet, but it has nothing like the melancholy of the songs, for they both give way to a lovely haunting warble; there is no other way to describe it. When you first hear it I must confess it takes a moment or two to realize that it comes from this fine large owl. The answer from the female is again higher pitched than that of the male.

The song can be heard from January until May, but after this month it gradually peters out, until by mid-July, when the young are almost vocal, it is a rare sound, only a storm and thunder bringing what seems to be a protest from the adult bird.

The nest is scarcely worthy of the name for it is usually in a hollow in a tree. There are seldom more than three eggs and they are at times almost round; they are white and usually laid in April.

The Tawny Owl's diet consists mainly of small rodents, especially rats and mice.

RAYMOND WATSON

The Wood Pigeon

Columba palumbus

The song of the Wood Pigeon is one of the sounds of the garden and countryside that I would miss very sadly. This fine grey bird will leap with beating wings and crack them in a sound which commands attention, meanwhile arching upwards in his courtship display. Then, with characteristic jerky flight, he wings back to the branch from which he rocketed earlier, and with swollen throat, yet barely open beak, he croons a remarkable series of phrases in the most familiar of garden voices. It sounds lazy, but this is due to the deep, almost soothing, way he offers his song. It speaks of summer days, with the heat of the fields under the influence of the noon sun, a sound calculated to have the listener slipping into a dreamy sleep. It begins thus '*Worg – worg – hoo – worg – worg – worg – coo – cor – oo – worg – worg – worg – worg – coo – caroo – worg*'. The last note ends abruptly as if the bird had been disturbed during his song.

I have mentioned the bird's barely open beak during this performance because I have had it under observation through my field glasses and have noticed time and time again that the big sound seems almost ventriloquial. I have noticed the same thing with the Cuckoo when it is calling.

Another note produced by the male Wood Pigeon is a snoring sound, which is one of his attempts to win over the female of his choice. He edges along a branch towards her, bowing deeply and advancing on his red legs, offering the deep, almost reverent sound, as if indeed he said, with great dignity, '*Good-Lord*', '*Good-Lord*'. This, by the way, is a sound which, if imitated, will bring this bird out of the tree like a rocket, to find and chastise an intruder. Countless times I have done this, and every time he will fly over, seeking the rival, never tiring of the chase. On many occasions I am in full view, but he takes not the slightest notice of me, so intent is he upon finding the non-existent rival. He never seems to suspect who is really mimicking his song.

Often this snoring sound can be a prelude to a song, as if, having assured the female Wood Pigeon that his affection is forever, he launches into the three-phrased song mentioned earlier. The song period will begin early in January and go on into October.

The Wood Pigeon's nest itself is not a work of art, so little material is used; in fact the eggs can sometimes be seen from below, and often some fall to the ground. Both birds gather the material, though the nest is built by the female. I have noticed more than once the eagerness of the male bird to help. After bringing small twigs he seems unable to wait until she reaches up for them. He will stand on her shoulders trying to hand down the twigs before she is ready for them.

There are two white eggs in each clutch, but the parents will undertake a fresh brood as soon as the young of the first are able to fend for themselves. Many times I have seen at least three broods during the season. The nestlings are not objects of great beauty. Often when I examine a nest and the two young lift their ugly heads, with whistling, begging sounds, I think of the nursery story of the Ugly Duckling. No duckling is ugly; nor is a gosling; and certainly no-one would dream of calling a cygnet ugly; but a nestling Wood Pigeon, known as a squab, can surely be described as ugly until it reaches adulthood. Then it becomes a most handsome bird, with superb plumage of blue-grey, with a white ring about the neck and a pinkish flush on its upper breast.

This big bird has no claim to be called the farmer's friend. Its crop is apt to be swollen with good things which the farmer did not plant for its benefit – clover, grain of various kinds, and the sweet tops of root crops. But I offer some defence, for the balance sheet is not one-hundred-per-cent bad. Charlock is a menace to any farmer, and the Wood Pigeon is very partial to it. It will also consume infant garden snails.

RAYMOND WATSON

The Meadow Pipit

Anthus pratensis

As a singer the Meadow Pipit cannot be considered as a rival to its near relation the Tree Pipit. But by the way it leaps to fluttering wings, and the long curving sweep it makes during the song flight, its display makes up for any shortcomings in the vocal performance.

When I performed regularly in the concert world I used every morning and afternoon to walk in the countryside surrounding the town where I was speaking. This gave me an opportunity to walk particularly in the uplands of Yorkshire and Lancashire, where I saw and listened to a number of birds which are not to be found in my home county of Suffolk. There was the Golden Plover, with his haunting '*Tur - pee - oor*', the Dunlin, with its shrill '*Pee - eer*', and the Red Grouse, whose almost human tones reminded me of old men grumbling. But the commonest bird of all in the northern uplands seemed to be the Meadow Pipit. I hardly moved a step without getting bitter complaints from them as they rose in their dozens protesting at my intrusion with shrill calls of '*Pee - pee - peet*' or '*Pee - peet*'. This call presumably explains the name Pipit.

The Cuckoo, which is closely linked with the Meadow Pipit, although a much larger bird, makes frequent use of the Pipit's nest for its offspring, so much so that a Welsh friend of mine in the concert world, who shared my interest in bird watching, told me that in Wales the Meadow Pipit was known as 'Gwas-y-gog', which means 'Cuckoo's serf'.

The Meadow Pipit is one of these Northern birds which is also to be found amongst the furze and heather on the Suffolk heathlands, and when my wife and I go to Dunwich hardly a moment passes without one of them rising swiftly from the heath with its thin little song '*Tee, teep, teep, teep, teep, teep, teep, teep, teep, teep*'. This is followed by a long sweep back to some shrub on which it perches, restlessly flicking its tail and wings before setting off again.

There is a second part to the song, which one doesn't always hear as the bird is apt to drop to earth suddenly and run along among the short grass and disappear. The second part of the song comes just before landing, and is '*Tit - tit - tit - tit - tit - tit - tit - tit - tit - tit - tit*', ending with a hard-sounding '*Teer - teer - teer - teer - teer - teer - teer*'. Its song is certainly by no means as beautiful as that of its more talented cousin the Tree Pipit. There always seem to be plenty of Meadow Pipits in the air or perched on the heather at Dunwich, but they are not easy to see until they complain about one's presence with a peevish '*Pee - peet*' or at times a harsh '*Sissick*', very similar to the flight call of the Pied Wagtail.

The nests of these small heathland birds are objects of great skill, which is not readily appreciated unless one examines a nest after the nesting season is over. The nest is marvellously camouflaged so as to merge with the surrounding heather. The small, tidy saucer that is the nest is made of teased-out grass, especially the wild heathland grass, to which a wall of moss is added. In this are laid four eggs of varying shades of dirty white, bearing a profusion of dark brown markings, so many as to create a uniform brown colouring.

The Meadow Pipit, though really a heathland bird, visits our garden for a day or two during the late autumn, when the cry of '*Pee - peet*' announces its presence. Incidentally, I suggest that the reader takes note of the difference between the hind toe of this bird and that of the Tree Pipit, as portrayed so skilfully by Raymond Watson.

RAYMOND WATSON

The Tree Pipit

Anthus trivialis

Vocally the Tree Pipit is one of the most gifted of British wild birds, yet apart from people who are especially interested in bird song it is little known. As a singer, in my opinion, it should rank with the Nightingale, the Blackbird, the Thrush and the Sky Lark.

Like so many of the singers whose melody makes the dawn chorus such a wonderful experience, it is a summer visitor to Britain, arriving during April. After a day or two of display, the cock chooses a mate, and after a period of courtship during which the lovely melody reaches perfection, they prepare for nesting. From the end of April or the beginning of May, according to the weather, the male Pipit sings constantly.

When I lived in Ipswich I used to walk down Spring Road, over which a high viaduct carries trains to and from Felixstowe and Lowestoft. Despite the roar of passing trains a pair of Tree Pipits used to nest on the embankment - surely one of the oddest nesting places for such a relatively uncommon wild bird. In spring, after the roar of a passing train had subsided, I used to watch the bird rise from its nest and pour out its song over the roof-tops of Ipswich. The Pipit was so untroubled by the cacophony of the passing trains that it returned to the embankment each year to raise a family. As I stopped in the street below I suppose onlookers thought me to be a railway buff watching he trains go by on the branch line. Little did they realize that my interest was in listening to the exquisite song of a wild bird whose name probably few of them had ever heard of. Whenever I hear its song nowadays, in less unusual surroundings, there comes to my mind the image of that high, bleak viaduct, above which a bird seemed to be singing its heart out, just for me.

There was another rather surprising place where I used also to go to listen to the Tree Pipit, and that was on the outskirts of the famous RAF aerodrome at Martlesham. Before the 1939-45 war I used to camp there alone, weekend after weekend, sleeping in a small bivouac tent. At night Little Owls and Nightjars kept up a discordant duet, but as the sunlight made its way through the Scots pines and birches I would peer out of the canvas opening of my tent through the heather and gorse, trying to pick out the Tree Pipit rising some fifty feet or more into the sky, and then, with wings and tail held rigid, floating down into a tree singing: '*Tee - seet - tee - seet - tee - seet - tee - seet - chip - chip - chip - chip - seet - seet - seet - seet - seet - seet - deer - deer - deer - deer - deer - deer*'. These last few notes were so glorious that they seemed to resound even after the bird had settled in the tree. During the war years I used to wonder how the Tree Pipit reacted to the roar of Wing-Commander Douglas Bader and his fellow fighter-pilots making their sorties into the sky from the same place.

Other notes sounded by this bird range from anger to alarm. Sometimes I could detect a single note not unlike that of Goldfinches when they quarrel. And if a Hawk came and perched on a telegraph pole the male Tree Pipit would utter a sharp '*Kip*'. The Hawk, of course, paid not the least attention.

The nesting season for Tree Pipits is from late May until mid-June. Through my field glasses I have watched the young being fed on many occasions. They seem to have a liking for grasshoppers which are abundant on the land where I have watched them. There are also a lot of spiders about, and I fancy they go the same way as the grasshoppers.

The nest is, as with Sky Larks, Wood Larks, and the other Pipits, on the ground. You should look for it on heaths, in clearings in woods, and on hillsides where there are scattered bushes. Often the nest is under bracken. The eggs vary considerably in ground colour and in markings. Some are so dark as to be almost red; others are so heavily covered with splashes and marks of a dark brown as almost to obscure the ground colour.

RAYMOND WATSON

The Lesser Redpoll

Carduelis flammea cabaret

One of the most popular of visiting birds as far as our garden is concerned is the Lesser Redpoll, a member of the Finch family which comes to the garden with fair regularity. The attraction is, I am certain, the number of silver birch trees whose massive heads present an undeniable attraction.

This little bird measures but four and three-quarters of an inch and its antics when flying over the birch trees are a joy to watch. It has a flight pattern that is very much its own, for although it is undoubtedly a finch, with its bounding flight, it has its own interpretation of how it should be tackled. It will make loops and circles high above the tops of the trees, and at other times it will make what I can only describe as 'figure-of-eight' loops and circles, quite unlike the larger finches in flight. There is also about this little creature's flight an almost pixie-like attitude. If ever a bird displayed a joy of living, it is in the flight of this small happy Redpoll.

Vocally, it is as lively a bird as it is possible to hear, for it is seldom quiet. It will greet a neighbour with the contact call which to me sounds like a gentle '*Morrie*', louder than the similar call of the Willow Warbler, and used more frequently. It is a most friendly call, and the other bird will respond, until the sequence of calls produces an elfin quality.

Another call, which is not so amiable, is the note when the bird quarrels with an intruder. This is a dry almost insect-like '*Sheeze*'. Most certainly it is an anger call.

It will sing on the wing, and the performance seems to me to be better than when the bird is perched, for there is about the song-flight an almost child-like quality that has care-free lilts. There are times when this is lacking, but mostly it holds a kind of 'joy of living'. If you whisper these notes they should give an excellent idea of the song: '*Cha - cha - cha - cha - peeree*'. The '*cha - cha*' notes are also used without the concluding '*perree*'; they are then just flight notes.

The food is both insect and vegetable. The bird will take aphides as well as small caterpillars; I have watched it at work on the wayfaring trees which at times are covered with black flies. The Redpoll also likes the seeds of birch and elder.

With us this little bird begins to sing during the early days of April, and we hear it until at least the first days of September. I am not able to say with conviction that it nests in our garden, and to be honest I doubt if it does; the appearance of the young would be sufficient evidence, and we do not see them. The Greenfinches and Chaffinches as well as the Goldfinches bring their young into the garden to feed, and the sight of masses of seeding cornflowers would undoubtedly prove an attraction to Redpolls and their young.

I have sometimes watched these small birds nesting and attending to the needs of their families. I have found eggs in the nests in May: they are a pale blue with a sprinkling of red markings. Some will have fewer marks while others will have the markings crowded at the larger end. The number of eggs varies, but I have found as many as six in one nest.

The Redpoll is an unaccountable little bird as far as its nesting arrangements are concerned. I have found a nest in a hawthorn hedge no more than eight feet up, yet one nest was pointed out to me high in an alder; so it is not easy to be exact about their sites.

A point to make about this small finch is its lack of fear of man. If I am standing under the birch trees on which it is feeding it will continue to pick at the catkins regardless of my presence.

To sum up, this small, happy bird is a beneficial species and should be protected at all costs. When I was a boy men used to trap it in hundreds and sell it as a cage bird in order to train it to draw water from a tiny well situated at the bottom of the cage: hence one of the local names for this bird is 'draw-water'.

RAYMOND WATSON

The Redstart

Phoenicurus phoenicurus

This small but very beautiful bird haunts areas which provide nesting holes such as old farm buildings, old trees, even ancient abbey ruins. I have seen it in gardens which were large and well cared for but which had out-houses where the stone work had fallen away or left gaps in the old mortar which provided snug retreats for well-hidden nests. Among the attractions for me of this bird are not only its neat, trim appearance but its nest, which though it is in a hole, will not have the tell-tale untidiness of those of the House Sparrow or the Starling. Quite often the only clue that birds are in residence is the emergence of the male bird, who will appear quite suddenly to confront the human intruder with notice to 'move on, please'. This is a single note which, although it attracts attention at once, is not an irritable note but carries in its sweetness a touch of appeal, fanciful as this may seem. I have heard it on many occasions and have written it down many times, but over the years have not had to change the description: '*Looick, looick*'.

Another call, which is more of a contact call than the one previously mentioned, is so wonderfully plaintive that one evening when I was near Nacton, in Suffolk, I heard what I was prepared to swear was the call of either a Willow Warbler or a Chiffchaff. It came from above where I sat below an old holly tree that had been struck by lightning and had one of its main branches torn away. This had left a gap that the weather had worked into. A Woodpecker had tried to dig into it to make a nest tunnel. What had happened after that I could not know, but a pair of Redstarts had found it to be ideal, and had nested there. The call I had heard came from the male bird, who flicked his red tail upwards and sideways in pantomime. When the female came out of the hole in the holly I was treated to a display of tail-fanning and flirting which was charming.

The call to which I referred came at intervals, and sounded to me like '*Looie*', a pause, and again '*Looie*'. I believe that today I am able to tell which is which when I hear a Chiffchaff, a Willow Warbler or a Redstart calling, but I would not like to gamble on it.

The song is like no other, for in its swift brightness, that sometimes carries a Robin-like lilt, it hurries the phrase towards the end, which is very abrupt. I have used a memory phrase over the years and have discussed it with several ornithologists who have agreed that it is a good description of the three-second burst of song. I have written it as '*Why don't you try to follow the rippling river?*' The river note is most abrupt. Anyone who makes a whispering imitation of that phrase may have captured the song of the Redstart and be able to identify it when they hear it. The points to bear in mind are its brightness and its race to completion.

As far as the eggs are concerned, I can recognize their colour, for many times I have watched both parents bring out of the holes shells of the empty eggs and drop them in the bracken nearby. They are a lovely greenish-blue. The number I do not know; but I have read that sometimes the birds will produce as many as six in the single clutch.

The Redstart is a summer visitor to our area, and I rarely see it, or, should I say, hear it, before the first week in May. I am sure it has been with us before that date, but the display to establish territory builds up as time goes on and only when the females arrive are there continuous bouts of singing.

Over the years I have collected many local names of this attractive little bird, and I would ask the reader to compare these names with Raymond Watson's painting. Here are one or two examples: 'Whitecap' – a reference to the white forehead, 'Red-Tail', 'Bran-Tail', 'Fire-Flirt', 'Fiery-Bran-Tail', 'Red-Fiery-Bran-Tail'; all bearing witness to the accuracy of the observers. The common name of 'Redstart' refers, as do all those local names, to the fiery red of the upper part of the tail.

The Robin

Erithacus rubecula

Each year a pair of Robins build their nest in our garage, on a girder. The first time they chose as their site the open mouth of a polythene bag that lay on the girder. I was worried lest when the eggs were laid they would roll out of the opening in the bag, so I gently pushed back the foundations of the nest a few inches, for safety's sake. Immediately the birds built another foundation in front of the first. Assuming that they had not got the message, I eased the new nest back alongside the first. To my amazement they built a third nest in front of the other two. I accepted their decision, and henceforth had to wash the roof of the car almost daily.

The birds bore me no ill-will, for as soon as the eggs were laid the cock began to sing with typical sweetness. (Mind you, this may have been partly due to the delicious diet we provided – a special soft-billed food mixed for us by our friend in Cleethorpes; and woe betide any other Robins who joined the party.)

The sites of Robins' nests, as most folk know, are many and varied. An old kettle, flung into a hedge, may provide shelter, and the sight of six reddish eggs, marked with white, in that strange home, is one of the marvels of bird life.

It puzzles me that the song of the Robin is not as well known as that of the Thrush or Blackbird. Perhaps this is because the Robin is so easily recognized by its red breast that its song gets overlooked. I know the phrases so well, having sung them hundreds of times in duet with the cock. Of course, he had no idea it was a human being who was accompanying him in his *'Sin – sin – tilly – lee – lee'* sung with beak wide open and red breast puffed out as he drew himself to his full height in the normal routine of challenge. The red breast is for intimidation; had I been another Robin a battle royal would have occurred.

The first phrase is followed by *'Wee – oo –*
till – lay – tee – or – less – still – lee'. But there is so much variation in the phrases that it is not possible to give an exact impression, as it would be with the song, for instance, of the Yellowhammer or the Chaffinch. There is also a weeping note, so incredibly thin that some ears might not catch it at all. It is a *'See – ee'*, very similar to that of the Blackbird, but not as loud. This, I am sure, is a distress call, made when hunger and danger combine.

There is also a special ticking note which we at home describe as the Robin 'winding up his clock'. It is a regular evening sound, sometimes an expression of alarm, but not as urgent as the sounds made when the bird is angry as well as alarmed. I remember commenting on a hissing sound as my wife and I were being shown round the great sanctuary for ducks and geese in Galloway. When I suggested to the warden that it was a Robin he was astonished. 'I often hear it', he said, 'but I thought it might be an angry cat hissing'.

No bird is more friendly than a Robin, or more useful in the garden. The Robin is not a fussy bird in its eating habits. Little escapes its bright eyes; even spiders and worms are eaten. I remember lifting a hydrangea shrub to find out what had caused it to wither. As I pulled the dead roots out of the hole I saw a grub, the larva of the cockchafer beetle, over an inch in length. Its head was reddish-brown, its body was revolting, almost Dracula-like in its curled shape. I did not know for a moment what to do with it; but I need not have concerned myself, for a Robin came down, dropped into the hole, and proceeded to dismember the horror, then to eat it. Afterwards it regarded me with a look which seemed to say 'I knew I could manage that.'

We are lucky that the Robin's song lasts for so long. With the exception of a few weeks in July and August hardly a day passes without this portly little bird winning our hearts with its trust and its tinkling song.

Visitors to the United States should bear in mind that the American Robin is a larger bird, a thrush, though it has a red and orange breast.

The Starling

Sturnus vulgaris

There can be few gardens that are not visited by this greedy, untidy bird in its search for food. It is a noisy bird, and, as far as its nesting arrangements are concerned, one of the most lazy, for any material will do as long as it can be welded into a semblance of a nest. Its favourite site is a hole in a roof or wall or tree, where the bird can be sure that some of the material can be stuffed into a tight bunch. Even then some of it will protrude and betray the site to everyone.

Having said all that, I must pay a tribute to the Starling as a parent. Anyone who has watched this bird feeding its squawking young will agree about its unending energy as it races across the garden to find food, and then races back, as if the most important thing in life is to feed its ungrateful family.

To watch the parent Starling at work while it searches for food is to realize that its services to agriculture and the garden are beyond price. It runs across the lawns, stops to examine a promising item, and then the lemon yellow beak is opened, and the hole in the ground is enlarged, all in the space of seconds. Then a probe reveals a grub, which is picked up and rushed across to the noisy offspring. Larvae such as wireworms and leatherjackets are consumed at an enormous rate; these are the larvae of the Click Beetle and Crane Fly.

Vocally the Starling does not rival such birds as the Blackbird and the Thrush, but because of its ability to imitate with uncanny skill the calls and the songs of some of the famous I would place this bird much higher than its own vocal powers might otherwise do.

I was on Belmont Moors some time ago with a keeper, and we both stood in wonder listening to the bubbling song of a Curlew. Then the keeper touched me gently on the arm and pointed with his chin to where a Starling was perched on a stone dyke, its beak wide open, its throat all spiky, the feathers standing out like a ruff. And then, with never a pause, it began to imitate the treble notes of the Golden Plover, a deep '*Turr - pee - oor - turr - pee - orr*', with such haunting beauty it was hard to believe the evidence of our eyes.

The Starling's own contribution to song is limited, for it will open its performance with the usual '*Weeil*' and then follow this with '*Whyee*', both shrill, almost ventriloquial, sounds. Then, as if on cue, it launches into mimicry. A Blackbird, Nuthatch, Peewit, Jackdaw, Moorhen, Coot and - without a pause - a baby crying, a barn door creaking, chicken clucking, a dog barking, all imitated with wonderful accuracy. Only two days before I began to write this, I went out into the garden where the snow lay deep. On the roof of the house, on a thick carpet of snow, a Starling was well into its selection of sounds of the countryside. Then it changed into an imitation of a bird which we do not find nesting in the British Isles, a Golden Oriole, who sings '*Weela - weeio - weela - weeio*'. This must have been one of the many Starlings who invade these islands during the winter, for it would never have heard the call of the Golden Oriole in Britain. Many times we have been puzzled to hear the mellow hoot of a Tawny Owl during bright sunlight; the originator always was the Starling.

Some books say the Starling will produce two broods in a season. This is not my experience, for when the noisy brown young are capable of flying they rarely fend for themselves; they use their wings to chase their parents whose feathers are showing signs of wear. After the parents leave our garden for the fields, where they congregate in masses, I cannot believe that they return to lay more eggs.

The pale blue eggs are normally five in number, though occasionally it is possible to find an extra egg upon the ground. This, I am sure, is due to an outstanding characteristic of the bird: everything it does must be achieved at top speed. If an egg is due, then it will be deposited on the ground if necessary.

70

The Stonechat

Saxicola torquata

What other name could we give to this neat, colourful bird, other than Stonechat? Anyone who listens to its dry call, '*Sak – sak*', cannot but liken the sound to the knocking together of two small stones. Even the local names, with but one exception, refer to that sound. 'Stonechatter', 'Stonesmith', 'Furze-Hacker'; while the other name, 'Blacktop', refers to the bird's black head.

The Stonechat is one of my favourites. It has never visited our garden, but we sometimes go to Dunwich cliffs where the jungle of tawny gold-blossomed furze is home ground for this handsome bird.

We find a clearing in which we park the car, lower the windows, and listen. Soon, amid a medley of the voices of Linnets, Sand Martins, Yellowhammers and Whitethroats there comes the unmistakable sound of '*Sak – sak*', as hard and as dry as dust. A Stonechat is protesting, and it is our presence at which he protests. Soon we spot him perched on a finger of furze, in full view, bobbing and calling his protest. The Stonechat is a great one for bobbing up and down. He is not bowing to the visitor; it is part of his nervous make-up. In a while he is off again across the common, only to rest on another branch of furze.

Most wild birds, when they are perched and the cares of a family have been attended to, seem to like to have five minutes' peace. They will perch low down upon their legs and observe their surroundings with complete calm. But the Stonechat is one of the world's restless creatures; it is never still. It is either scratching or looking round and shifting on its perch. A human companion such as that would drive one crazy. Here is his voice when he gives way to distress or exasperation, for he is an expert at complaining: '*Wee – sak – sak, wee – sak – sak – sak – sak – sak – sak*', no more than three seconds in duration, but the point is well made; we are not welcome!

After a while we are treated to a burst of song, though it takes a keen ear to realize that this indeed is the song of the Stonechat. He bobs and he bows, and he scratches behind his ear, and then without a pause he sings. It is a hard little voice, though it is possible at times to detect some quite sweet notes in it. But you have to listen and get to know the song before you can isolate the sweet notes, which are delivered so hurriedly, and yet so hesitantly. The full song is '*Site – site – sak – kitty – kitty – chah – cah*'. If you whisper those sounds it is possible to get some idea of the song. While he is singing it he will often rise up to a fair height – he has a darting flight not unlike that of the common Whitethroat.

Back on his perch his attitude reminds me of the restlessness of the Spotted Flycatcher: his head is seldom still; he looks upward, downwards, sideways, always on the move, and woe betide a careless moth who decides to move to a shady area.

As far as nesting arrangements are concerned, there is great activity from both male and female. The nest is mostly made on the ground, but we have found two nests that were about a foot above ground and on the branch of a tough furze bush. Those on the ground are works of art, for they are often woven with a kind of approach tunnel, similar to the nest of the House Sparrow when it nests in a tree. The eggs are pale greenish-blue. We have never found more than four, but whether this is the usual total I cannot say. When the young hatch out from the eggs, the devotion of the parents is remarkable. No winged insect has a chance of life while these lively little birds feed their young; caterpillars are fed regularly, and I used to wonder where the young managed to put them, for the to-and-fro journeys of their parents seem almost continuous. Once, however, after watching through our field glasses, we decided to wait a while, and we crossed over to take a look. The mystery was solved, for on the lip of the nest were a dozen or more small caterpillars lying there limp and lifeless as in a larder.

RAYMOND WATSON

The Mistle Thrush

Turdus viscivorus

This is without any doubt the most alert, and also bossy, of the birds that visit our garden. I watch it from the conservatory as it races across the grass in short bursts of running, and then suddenly stops, stands bolt upright, while it searches the grass for the red tip of a worm which has thrust its head out to savour the dampness of the morning. The Mistle Thrush is a fine big powerful bird, much larger and lighter in colour than its smaller cousin, the Song Thrush. It is much more heavily marked than the smaller bird: indeed the markings are spots, quite large ones compared with the streaks of the Song Thrush.

It seldom wastes its time. After one of those hurried rushes there is just a quick dip of the head sideways; and then if the worm is too quick or the bird was mistaken it is away again on twinkling legs. The Mistle Thrush is indeed a wild bird in the true meaning of the word. It will not tolerate familiarity but is soon on its way with that rattling alarm note not unlike the rattles of football supporters.

The song, which is of two quick phrases, is sung from January to the end of May, though if there is a chance of a thunderstorm it will break out into what sounds like protest at having to resume the wild notes. The full song, which I have had written down since childhood, has to my hearing changed little. Few of these big birds seem inclined to do more than vary the two phrases very slightly. My memory phrase is '*Bye - bye - Dorothy - Dorothy - behave*' sung over and over again. If you whisper those sounds you can offer the best interpretation of that wild song, which incidentally has earned for the bird one of its most accurate local names, that of 'Storm Cock'. When there is a prospect of stormy weather you will hear that wild whistled song of protest, as if the bird, perched high as it almost always is, were voicing its resentment. The Mistle Thrush is a most quarrelsome

bird, especially with others of its own kind. Smaller birds come in for much bullying if they intrude into the nesting domain. The nest is almost always placed on a fork in a tall tree, though I have once or twice found it in the crown of a hawthorn hedge. The nest is typical of the bird, an untidy mass of grass, twigs, moss, and oddments of soft items it might gather from household rubbish. The interior is unlike that of its cousin the Song Thrush, for that bird will line its nest with mud or dung. The Mistle goes one better: the mud lining is covered with teased-out dried grass. The eggs are unlike those of the smaller bird: they are usually creamy, with a reddish wash, though sometimes the ground colour is a washed blue. Incidentally, those I found nesting in the top of the hawthorn were of this ground colour. The Mistle Thrush will produce two broods a year, especially if the year opens mildly, for the bird goes to nest early.

During the winter it will take to the fields, and to attract it into the gardens again it will be necessary to cut up apples, whatever their condition - the Mistle Thrush is not fussy - and spread them as far apart as possible, so that you will be able to observe the bird at its meal. It will sit there until it is hungry again, and the only bird who would dare to challenge it is the Fieldfare, a winter-visiting thrush.

As I have said, this bird is a most jealous rival to antagonize. I doubt whether there is another of our wild birds who reacts more swiftly to the sound of a rival within its nesting territory. I sometimes say to my wife, 'Our friend the Mistle Thrush is doing his best to frighten away interlopers. I will have a song-battle with him'. So I wait until he pauses, which he often does; then I whistle his two phrases back at him, and the effect is almost electrical. A moment of silence then back comes the answer. Within a few seconds he is off with a swift-winged flight to seek the intruder. He will choose the highest tree in order to find out just where the rival is; then, as if impatient, he wings back to his previous post and we have a right old battle.

74

RAYMOND WATSON

The Song Thrush

Turdus ericetorum

Its number of local names, such as 'Mavis', 'Drish', 'Thrusher' and 'Whistling Dick', all bear witness to its vocal powers. And I doubt if there is a bird more popular with gardeners not only for its lovely songs but also for its unending pursuit of garden pests. Every gardener recognizes that short perky run, followed by the sideways cocking of the head in search of the worm. It is a mistaken idea that the bird is *listening* to the worm, for the worm makes no sound. The bird's purpose is simply to get into position for the grab and the upwards jerk as the worm tries to resist.

If the quarry is a snail, which is hoping to retreat into the safety of its shell, the Thrush has learnt over the years how to lift the snail by the lip of its shell, carry it to a stone or path, and batter it out of house and home.

The mating season begins at the first let-up in wintry weather, and it often heralded by the male bird announcing from the highest available point that the nesting site has been chosen. The sheer power of that whistle is almost unbelievable, and I have often heard it from as far distant as a quarter of a mile. The song often begins with '*Sweetheart - sweetheart - sweetheart*'. Then the warning note to rivals: '*Beat - you, beat - you, beat - you*'. This is followed by other calls: '*So - I - did, so - I - did, so - I - did*' and '*Hear - me, hear - me - be - quick - be - quick, be - quick*'. Then comes '*Look - behind - you - look - behind - you*' and, as a finale, '*Take - heed, take - heed, take - heed*'. Not for nothing is this fine bird called 'the talking Thrush'.

The alarm note can be a short '*Choop - choop*', which is often lengthened into a shriek of alarm notes run together, not unlike the brisk alarm notes of the Blackbird, but harder and higher-pitched. Another note, used on the wing, is, I am sure, a contact note. It is also used when the bird is disturbed while feeding: just one short '*Seet*' and it is away.

For the nest, which may be in a thick hedge or bush or the lower branches of a tree, the female makes a solid foundation of mud, worked up into a cup shape, reinforced with grass, roots and twigs, cemented with mud or cow dung and smoothed to such a high degree that the six or more eggs can lie snug and dry. As with most eggs, their colour varies a little, a vivid blue, spotted, sometimes heavily, sometimes more lightly, with brown or black.

If they are undisturbed, Thrushes will remain faithful to single nesting site. In our garden one bird build beneath the dovecote every year for several years. Once, after a very mild winter, it nested very early and we watched it build three nests, the last one on top of the second.

It is amusing to watch what must be the education of the young Thrush by the adults, and, incidentally, it is a lesson in patience to many a human parent. How many would tolerate perpetual harassment by clamouring young during mealtimes? I have watched a parent feed a noisy fledgling who screamed through a full beak for more, and then ran with fluttering wings to chase the poor adult bird who had made contact with the red tip of another worm. Needless to say the worm won the day, for the fledgling Thrush rushed in to receive it before the food was ready. Such was the parent bird's acceptance of such an interruption that it merely hurried across the grass to seek others.

The good this splendid bird and its kind do for agriculture is immeasurable.

No man or boy should lift his hand against the Thrush and the others of its kind. The wild bird has enough natural enemies without mankind adding to its troubles. Moreover its nest and eggs are objects of great skill and beauty, to be admired, not destroyed.

The Song Thrush is a friend and unpaid worker in the garden, as well as a marvellous singer, and if he or she sometimes takes a little fruit as bonus, remember that the fruit is not there for most of the year, but the Thrush is.

76

RAYMOND WATSON

The Blue Tit

Parus caeruleus

This tiny bird is one of the best-loved garden visitors, which, if encouraged, will render much service in its battles against greenflies, caterpillars and other garden pests. I will not attempt to describe the plumage, which is so superbly painted by Raymond Watson; it would be impossible to put into words the colours with which this tiny bird delights us when it arrives at the bird table. And its cheerful little song rings out across the garden from January to July, with a brief resumption of song at the end of August. There may also be a few outbursts during September.

I have likened the song many times to the sound of an elfin creature bowling a silver marble across a frozen pond. If this sounds fanciful, try to sing these notes, bearing in mind the ringing quality of the voice: '*Tee - ee - lilly - lilly - lilly - lilly - lilly - lilly*'.

Vocally it has a variety of notes; indeed all the Titmice who visit the garden are not content with just a single song; and listeners who are interested in the variety of garden voices will find much to fill their notebooks. One call is '*Tee - tee - bee*', and it rings out again and again; it is a contact note. There is another which sounds to me as if the bird is feeding, and just keeping in touch, however odd that may sound to those who have not studied bird voices. It is a bright '*Tee - tee - tit*'. When the birds are mating they indulge in sounds which are often more hissing than any kind of a whistle, but with much wing-shivering, especially upon the part of the female – they keep this up while playing follow-my-leader. Then there is the alarm note which scolds the intruder: '*Churrer - did - did - did*'.

The Blue Tit's natural nesting places are in garden hedges and in holes in trees, walls and drain-pipes. In our garden we have a number of nesting-boxes, and Blue Tits take readily to these. Two years ago a pair nested in one on a silver birch tree, and while the BBC filmed for the 'Gardener's World' programme the birds went in and out with only a mild protest of '*Churrer - did - did - did*'. In their beaks they brought a variety of food such as green caterpillars and greenflies, with such energy that the camera man was fascinated. Incidentally, his huge camera was only three yards away from the nesting area.

Indeed, the Blue Tit, like other Titmice and the Robin and the Blackbird, seems to have struck up a specially friendly relationship with the human race, and is traditionally grateful for the halved coconuts that are hung out for it during cold spells in the winter.

Such a popular little bird must have many local names, and I will mention only 'Billy-Biter', a reference doubtless to the reaction to an inquisitive finger making its way into the nesting hole, 'Blue-Tom', 'Pick-Cheese', 'Tit-mall', 'Blue-Ox Eye' and 'Bluebonnet'.

The number of eggs they lay each time they nest makes one wonder why we do not see greater numbers of Blue Tits invading the gardens. Many survive to fly from the nest, but somehow the numbers the following year do not seem to increase. Where have the others gone? Possibly it is a wise move by nature to ensure that the mortality rate keeps them within normal numbers.

The eggs are, as you can imagine, tiny; they are white with red spots of reddish-brown mostly at the larger end. I look into each nest-box only once, and then I leave the parents to their task. What energy they have for not only do they feed on caterpillars and greenflies but they still come to the bird table for scraps of fat and rolled oats for the young.

When the nesting season draws to a close there is a bedlam of pleading cries from the fledglings, who follow their parents round the garden and the adjoining fields with what seems an endless chain of open beaks, all with the same message, '*Me, Me, Me, Me*'.

The young birds have the same pattern of plumage as their parents but it is less bright, and there is a touch of green which will become blue later.

RAYMOND WATSON

The Coal Tit

Parus ater

This is the smallest of the family of Titmice, and is one of my favourites, for its busy, almost frantic, search for food is not only amusing to watch but tells us that it is doing a lot of good in the garden. Watching it at work makes me feel ashamed that I am sitting idly watching when a large garden needs my attention. I often wonder how so much energy can be generated in so tiny a creature while some of the larger birds, such as the Wood Pigeon, move about the branches in a lazy sort of way.

As you see in Raymond Watson's painting, the Coal Tit is not only smaller than the Blue Tit but can be distinguished from it by its jet-black crown. Like the other Tits it is extremely agile, almost acrobatic, in its movements as it attacks a hanging bag of nuts. The Coal Tit is also a very inquisitive and contentious bird, and if it becomes aware of a rival it will cross the space between and demonstrate its disapproval by sounding its anger call in no uncertain tone as if to say 'This is my cabbage patch, friend'.

Vocally the Coal Tit has all the variety of the other Tits. One call which intrigues me is a clear 'Knee-deep', a very high-pitched call and one that apparently other birds cannot resist. If I copy this call the Coal Tit is across the garden in a second, searching for the intruder. In the spring we hear the song which is a repeated '*Tee - bee - tee - bee - tee - bee - tee - bee - tee - bee - tee - bee*'. There is also another song which sounds like '*Hee - say - hee - say - hee - say - hee - say*'. It is quite different from the '*Tee - bee*' song. There is also a trilling kind of note: '*Sid - ee - sid - ee - sid - ee - sid - ee - sid - ee - sid - ee*', a continuous sound. It might easily be mistaken for a song, but I am sure it is for contact purposes, a bird calling to its mate as it searches the pine trees. I watch it while it climbs the bark of the pines as skilfully as a Treecreeper, though it has not the same jerk-ing movement. Also it will sometimes sing a song that for a moment foxes me into thinking that I am listening to a Treecreeper. Its movements are so swift that I wait for it to re-appear, and then I realize that I have been mistaken.

The nest is always in a hole in a tree or in a bank or even in a wall, where it will weave all kinds of soft material such as moss (there is no shortage of this in our garden) into a thick foundation often two inches in depth, plus feathers, all in all a nest with such a soft, comfortable lining that it is no surprise that the female will lay as many as nine eggs. Ornithological colleagues have told me that at times there can be as many as twelve or more. All I can say to them is that two females must have agreed to share the home, though when watching how these little birds treat an intruder it must be very unlikely. The eggs are very similar to those of the other Tits, being white with a fine freckling of red.

This bird, as I have said, is highly beneficial in the garden, for most of its food consists of insects and their eggs, and I have seen it at work on weed patches eating seeds of thistle-heads. As we have more than our share of marsh-thistle in our garden these little birds are very welcome to their ration.

Coal Tits also like to get their share of the peanuts which we hang up in bags and any other food we put out on the bird table. As often as not, however, they will be driven off by those bullies of the bird table the Great Tit and the Greenfinch, who will land on the table and spread their wings in a threatening gesture. The Coal Tit, however, it not entirely defeated. If you watch it carefully you will see if fly to an adjoining tree where it will play a waiting game, watching the larger birds until they fly away to digest one of the larger nuts. The little Coal Tit will then be back in a flash, pecking away in frantic haste - such haste, in fact, that it will probably drop to the ground some fragments for which a lurking Dunnock is duly grateful. In fact a variety of birds have parts to play in this peanut pantomime.

The Great Tit

Parus major

The name stems from the Anglo-Saxon, in which the word 'tit' denotes something small. The word 'mouse' has nothing to do with the little four-legged creature whom we know by that name. The Anglo-Saxon word 'mase' denotes a small *bird*. This can be confusing if you happen to live in Suffolk. One day I was watching an old thatcher who was showing me how to make hurdles. He remarked: 'Jest now I see a mase run under them faggots'. He was not referring to a bird but to a field mouse.

The Great Tit is the daddy of the family, being a comical bully, though the smaller Tits do not find him comical. The Great Tit is often referred to as a Tom Tit, but it has a variety of local names as well, such as 'Bee-biter', 'Black-bonnet', 'Joe Bent', 'Saw-Sharpener', 'Pick-Cheese', 'Sit-ye-Down' and 'Tom Collier'.

As with the Blue Tit, Marsh Tit and Coal Tit, the Great Tit takes readily to a nesting-box, which should have an opening on the north-east sheltered from the wind, not more than an inch and a quarter wide, or else Starlings will try to get in. All the Titmice family will put down a layer of some nesting material, with a lining of two inches, and felted to such an extent that when I clear out the nest-box after the nesting season is over I find it is packed as deeply with underfelting as any under the carpets in the house. The eggs of the Great Tit are white with small reddish spots, and there are often as many as eight or nine to the clutch.

As most bird-lovers know, the Tits are particularly fond of coconuts, as well as bags of nuts, from which they hang with acrobatic skill. Some books mention that there is often a second brood, but the Tits in our garden seem to produce only one. When the young begin to use their wings they follow their parents through the shrubs and trees clamouring for greenflies and small caterpillars.

It isn't easy to say which of the numerous phrases the adult birds use is the most characteristic song. The most common is the strident spring cry of '*Beat - you - beat - you, beat - you*'. This is the cry which is responsible for many false telephone calls. Times without number I switch off the mower to make sure whether it is the telephone or the Great Tit who is calling me.

I have a list of other calls and phrases which I have heard the Great Tit utter during the years. There is the well-known '*Pink - pink*', which is supposed to be an imitation of the similar call of the Chaffinch; it is a rather harder sound, and is often followed by a slurred alarm cry when it becomes '*Pink - pink - cha - cha - cha*', something which we never hear from the Chaffinch.

Another call of the Great Tit is '*Sat - sat - ee - sat*', and yet another is '*fee - poy*', most plaintive, with a note of query in it. Then there is '*Pin - pin - pin - pin, chee - bur - chee - chee - bur - chee*'. This, I am sure, is a challenge when a rival is hunting in the resident's nesting site. Another alarm is '*Pin - pin - cha - cha - cha*', which is often used when the Tit is not too sure of the identity of the intruder. Again, '*You - de - you - de - you - dee*', which is not quite as strident as the '*Beat - you*' sequence. Finally, there is a '*Sin - dee - dee - sin - dee - dee*', which we hear during the resumption of song during the autumn. These are but a few of the collection of songs I have recorded since boyhood, but there are others – though it would confuse the beginner to mention more than those most commonly used by this talkative bird, which not only enlivens the garden with its bright colours but is also one of the gardener's chief allies.

One cannot say, though, that the Great Tit is welcome at the bird table, as far as the smaller birds are concerned. The tiny Coal Tit is bullied unmercifully, and seldom gets an opportunity of feeding without disturbance. Even if there is more than enough room for the two birds, the Great Tit is certain to arch its wings and threaten the smaller bird.

RAYMOND WATSON

The Long-tailed Tit

Aegithalos caudatus

But for its tail, which is fully three inches in length, this tiny bird could claim to be the smallest bird in Britain. The body length, from the tip of the stubby little beak to the root of the tail, is only two and a half inches.

Where I live we have visits from these lovely birds almost daily. It is only during a severe winter that they desert us, doubtless to search for food at the edges of woods where undergrowth hides much of the insect food on which they exist. A bitter winter deals harshly with them not only for the lack of insect food but also for the inability of their tiny bodies to stand up to frost. In our dovecote I have seen at least fifteen of these pathetic creatures huddled together for warmth.

As far as song birds are concerned they do not rank very highly, but I should miss not only their dry little song, but many of the contact notes which ring out daily in the spring. The song is just a brief sounding of rippling notes, which to my hearing is a mixture of the calls, though the quivering of the wings tell me that the male bird is at least attempting a song. In words it is not easy to convey all that I hear; but if the reader will try to whisper '*Sirr – ur – see – sirr – ee – surr*', combined with what can only be described as water bubbling, it will convey some idea. The contact call is high-pitched and usually of four notes, '*Tee – tee – tee – tee*', continually uttered. The birds are never still; they search each twig, each dried and dead leaf which the winter may have missed, where some insect in its larva form has hoped to pass the winter in safety.

There is one other phrase which I have often mistaken for a song, but this I hear only when a Kestrel sweeps over the garden. The Kestrel has no interest in these tiny creatures, and is merely intent upon watching the banks of the ditches for field mice or the voles that haunt the area. At times the Kestrel will alight upon one of the posts nearby and watch with steady concentration for any movement which might suggest a meal. In so doing it starts a panic among the small birds. While the Blackbird and others noisily abuse the inoffensive Kestrel, the tiny Long-tails shrill these notes: '*Thittup – sup – sup*'.

This little bird must be the easiest one to decoy, for it cannot resist those four call notes. When they are searching the twigs on our Lombardy poplars they call to one another constantly, and if I want to show a visitor what they look like at close quarters I have only to imitate those four notes and they shoot and perch in the nearest tree seeking their neighbour. It is not rivalry that prompts their response but companionship. They are the friendliest of little birds, and endless conversationalists. Their '*Stirrup*' call punctuates the '*Tee – tee – tee – tee*' calls.

As for the nest of the Long-tailed Tit, though I have seen many in the fastnesses of gorse commons, I have yet to find any trace of its nesting in our garden, though they would be most welcome. I have a wild patch covered with briar and bramble, and one day, if I am lucky, a pair of these small birds may come and build there that small masterpiece which is about the length of a human hand and is stippled with moss, with a hole at the side towards the top. I call it a masterpiece but no human hand could build anything like it. I have read that over two thousand feathers have been found in the make-up of a nest. While congratulating the patience of those who counted, my real admiration is reserved for the tiny architects who foraged far and near to procure such a number, plus the mossy covering of the nest. It is no wonder that country folks have coined so many local names for the creators of such a work of art. I have heard the bird called 'Bottle-Tit', 'Feather-Poke', 'Jack-in-the-Bottle', 'Pudden-Poke', and 'Oven-Builder'.

Often as many as ten little red-spotted white eggs are somehow packed into and hatched in that tiny nest.

84

The Marsh Tit

Parus palustris

The name of this bird is misleading, for the Marsh Tit is no more a bird of marshy territory than is the Wood Pigeon. We have the bird visiting our bird table daily and we certainly are not in marshy country. It is one of the most popular of our visitors because of its apparently fearless visits to the bird table. When I go out to fill the various receptacles with fresh peanuts the other birds fly off and wait a short distance away until I go back into the house. But the Marsh Tit ignores me. Perhaps he makes a turn of the head, with a look which plainly says 'Oh, it's you again'. Then he calmly selects a nut and wriggles it out of the mesh before he departs.

Mind you, peanuts are not the only items of food enjoyed by this bold bird. It will vie with the larger Great Tit in wresting the nutricious nuts from the broad face of a gigantic sunflower, and scold at its big rival until it has the nut firmly held in its small beak. Not until then will it dart away. It will hang upside down while clinging to a fragment of butcher's suet, and from this position battle with others of its family, even the Blue Tit. The language is well worth recording. It can be a slurred '*Pur - urr - urr - dic - dee*', and soon after this it will dig the tiny beak into the suet in such a comical manner that it is difficult not to believe that the Marsh Tit has an imp of mischief inside that little feathered frame.

This bird is a favourite with my wife, who says that it fears no one, not even the bullying tactics of the Great Tit. Until now, though we hear the soft '*Chick - a - dee - dee - dee*' call regularly throughout the year, and especially during the nesting period of April to June, it has never shown the slightest interest in our nest boxes, as others of the Tit family do.

Vocally, in addition to the '*Chick - a - dee - dee - dee*' calls, it has many others which it can use, and this is one of its attractions to us. There is the song which is at times so like the 'Chips' of a Canary: '*Sip - sip - sip - sip - sip - sip - sip*', clear and sweet; yet at other times it will offer '*Supee - supee - supee - supee - supee - supee*', the 'u' being as in 'sup', a fine clear double note which rings through the garden with all the apparent joy of living.

One Marsh Tit caught me out when I was a boy. I had entered in my notebook a call which I heard from the Marsh Tit as an abrupt '*Sit - u*', and after a second or so again the '*Sit - u*'. In my youthful ignorance I imagined that this was the sum total of the Marsh Tit's call notes; but the following week, when I was sitting waiting for a Stock Dove to answer me, I heard '*Pit - cha - cha*' and at once yet another, but this time it was '*Pit - cha - cha - cha*'. Oh dear, pride went before a fall; I had to add to my notes.

Another, much later, occasion when my pride took a beating was when I was in America and I noticed a bird that seemed to be a twin of our Marsh Tit. It was calling with regularity the '*Chickadee - dee*' notes, just as we hear in English woodlands. What a wonderful surprise! But my companion, an American gentleman who was knowledgeable about the birds of his country, said 'No Sir! The bird you are listening to at this moment is a Black-capped Chickadee, so named because of its call.' I had to admit my mistake, but the bird's plumage was not dissimilar to that of the English Marsh Tit, and indeed the two birds belong to the Paridae family. Oddly enough, this Black-capped Chickadee possessed very few calls compared with our Marsh Tit, but it had a song of two notes which were so plaintive that the listener could not but wonder. It was a gentle '*Phee - bee*'.

Nowadays I never state with conviction that a certain bird has only this or that, and I refrain from using the word 'never' of a wild bird, for surely the next time you watch or listen it will confound you. It is like saying that the female Cuckoo never calls the well-known '*Cuckoo*'.

Local names for the Marsh Tit include 'Coal-head', 'Smaller Ox-Eye' and 'Joe Bent'.

RAYMOND WATSON

The Treecreeper

Certhia familiaris

A pair of Treecreepers have set up their headquarters in my garden. They are as alike as two peas, being brown above and pure white below, especially the throat and the upper part of the breast. Unless the male bird sings, which thankfully he does from April to July, I have some difficulty in telling which is which.

Treecreepers are not great movers, not in the class of the Sky Lark or the Wood Lark; but if one's active life is spent almost entirely in short avenues between trees who needs more than a quick bounding flight like that of the Tits? The food is there. True, one has to probe for it in the crevices of the bark. Nature provides not only the grub or grubs but she also provides the tools with which to finish the job. The beak is ideal, curved and thin, a perfect tool for winkling out the hidden larva of some insect.

The nesting site this pair have discovered in our garden is in a big tree partially covered with the rampant climber known as a Russian vine. The bark is broken away in some places, and with great cunning these two birds have built a home in the gap. Even the Magpie who is such a menace to smaller birds has no clue as to where it is hidden.

The beauty of those eggs! Six: white, with reddish brown at the big end, like a halo. Not one of the eggs is bigger than the nail on my little finger. The nest is a work of art, and the female Treecreeper has only her beak with which to create it.

Their courtship is a joy to watch. It takes place in the willows over the pond; and, my word, the sounds one can hear then! But keen hearing is necessary. The male bird does all the chasing. The female has all the skill of her sex, and plays hard to get. His Lordship is so exasperated he just *whispers* those incredibly thin notes. Then they play ring 'a roses round and round the willows by the pond. Such is

their skill of dodging and twisting one is left wondering why their normal flight seems so 'uppy-downy', as if it were such a chore to fly. But in this courtship flight they are as expert as circus performers. What amuses me is that both birds do that wing-trembling act that is normally performed only by a hen bird when she begs for food from the male.

The sound that the male bird makes when he is chasing the hen is so high-pitched that it defies description. Another note, which both birds use, is a very sharp '*See - oo*'. When they are excited or the nesting site is invaded they run the notes together into a kind of a trill. It is a note used by many small birds in the spring when the Cuckoo is calling and happens to perch near a nesting site. One other note, which can be used as a call note, is a quiet '*Seet*'. This is used most frequently when the song season has finished; it is used during the feeding time when the two birds are searching for grubs. I am convinced that it is a contact note, for sometimes I have heard it when the bird is flying between the trees.

Their song is sometimes likened to the songs of the Goldcrest and the Hedge Accentor, but I cannot hear it without at once recognizing it as from the Treecreeper. The rhythm, for one thing, is always the same, even if, as sometimes happens, the bird seems to be a little bored with the monotony of the six or seven notes. It is still a thin, whispered '*Hee - hee - hee - this - is - mee*'. At times it may sound like '*Set - set - set, sissy - thee*', but the rhythm is the same.

As I write a Treecreeper is working its way up the big willow over the pond. It is not singing; it has worked its way past the nestbox I put there. I assume the bird is not interested. This surprises me, for this particular box would seem to me to be ideal for Treecreepers, as it is deep and long, with a wide top gradually tapering down to a narrow base. It very nearly imitates the shape which a Treecreeper seeks when it finds a gap behind loose bark on a tree in which to pack its nesting material. There's no accounting for taste!

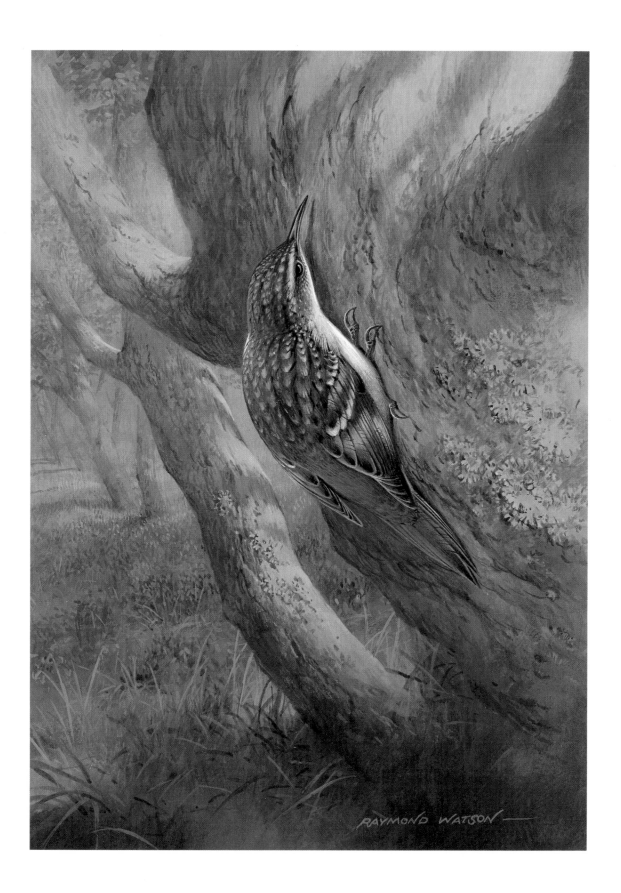

RAYMOND WATSON —

The Pied Wagtail

Motacilla alba

In 1947 I wrote for this bird this memory phrase: '*Chissit - chissit - chissit - cheffey - choyet - chissit*'. It is a bright little phrase with not much in the way of beauty; but the obvious joy it seems to give the singer makes up for what it lacks in performance. True, most of this phrase is made up of the call which can be heard all through the year when the bird runs down a lane or darts upwards in pursuit of a winged insect.

Many bird-watchers know how this bird will pause in its rapid twinkle-footed run, and leave its tail to continue to wag. Often the bird will announce its arrival on the lawn with this call: a sharp '*Chissit*', which it will repeat again and again as it runs across the grass in eager search for flies. It will dip its head to take an unwary insect, or leap on fluttering wings to take one which flies overhead. It is a very neat little bird, and to have one or two racing over the lawn adds to the pleasure of a garden. Raymond Watson has captured the attitude very well. It does not seem to have the variety of calls which so many of our resident wild birds possess; for example, the Chaffinch has a great number, and some of the Titmice family have a bewildering variety; but the Pied Wagtail seems to be content with just the song which begins during March and April.

I do not hear the song again until September. Through the autumn period of shortening days I hear it constantly singing; it will run along the ridging tiles of a building, pause a second while it shrills the brief song, and then off again, running down the tiles to capture an unfortunate fly. Then up on restless wings to overtake a passing insect, back to the tiles again, with the song almost as a punctuation of its movements. It is seldom still; the next second it is on the ground, running at top speed, a pause, then away again, with the call note of '*Chissit*' and the endless wagging of that long black, white-edged tail.

I sometimes hear its call note when crossing a busy street in a city. Indeed, even in London's West End it can be a common sound, and when I look up there it will be, running along a window sill, dipping to take some household fly which was intent upon finding its way into an office. Many times I have attracted amused glances from passers-by who no doubt wondered what the old white-headed man was looking at as he stood still on the pavement. This is where good hearing is so useful to bird-watcher. Nine times out of every ten you will hear a bird before you see it.

As far as its nesting requirements are concerned the Pied Wagtail is most attracted to holes. I have found a nest deep inside the broad hub of a rake wheel which leant against the wall of a barn. It is to the eternal credit of the farmer and his men that the bird reared two families in that hub, and woe betide any predator, farm cat included, who ventured near. I have also found a nest in a hole in a wall of an outside loo - not the most up to date of buildings - but the birds managed to bring up one family of seven young. Another was inside a faggot of sticks that were being harvested for pea-sticks. Needless to say they were not used for supporting peas that season. We had one Wagtail that lined anew the old nest of a Thrush which was in a mass of honeysuckle below the dovecote roof. For some reason the birds did not produce any eggs; we never knew what became of them. A pair did nest in an open-fronted nest-box, though whether or not they were the same pair we had no means of knowing. But the sight of that female Pied Wagtail's head, with its white crown showing plainly, was one of the pleasures of our garden that year.

The eggs are usually a goodly number, for often we find six, and once we found seven - a fine clutch of smoky-white eggs, with dark specks crowding the shell, and a few in a circle at the larger end, not unlike the crown of a Franciscan monk.

The food is almost exclusively insects.

90

RAYMOND WATSON

The Garden Warbler

Sylvia borin

This is one of the few wild birds of our gardens and open countryside that has virtually no distinguishing features. It has no prominent patches of colour, marks or streaks such as the dark eyestreak of the Nuthatch or the red face and breast of the Robin. The Garden Warbler has only its song; there is little else by which the observer can identify it. But goodness knows its name is perfect for it. It is indeed a superb Warbler, with a richness of song that surpasses that of most others, with the exception of its near relation, the Blackcap. Some of the latter will occasionally offer an indifferent performance, but my experience of the Garden Warbler, even during its first days after the long journey from its winter quarters, is that its song, rich, deep and prolonged, is a masterly effort.

The Garden Warbler arrives in my garden a week or so after the Blackcap. From the spinney comes a muttered warble, as if the hidden bird, lacking an opportunity of practice during the long flight from its winter quarters, is singing the melody from memory. It is almost perfect, except that the volume is not yet as strong as it will be in a day or so, when the bird will have chosen a nesting site.

I have written in the chapter on the Blackcap how, like the god Pan, it pipes a careless melody. The Garden Warbler, on the other hand, must have taken singing lessons from a brook passing under a small bridge. By contrast to that of the Blackcap, its song is a sustained burble and gurgle of deep melody. It is a song that took me ages to memorize and to write down, for no sooner had I written down the first two notes of the melody when what followed was of such quality and speed that I forgot what I had written. Now, after years of imitating the song, with the bird in attendance, I know it as well as I know the Lord's Prayer.

If you remember to whisper the notes with a sibilant sound you will have after a while an idea of the content, as well as the length, of the song. '*Wit - ur - why - dee - why - dor - did - ee - per - chur - did - ee - chur - chee - choy - did - it - per - tud - a - dud*'. This last note is deeper than the rest. And it is necessary to bear in mind when running over the song that it carries on at a continuous burble. There is no hesitation; it hurries along until it reaches the last notes, which, as I say, are deeper than the others.

There is an alarm note which is not unlike the dry '*Sek - sek*' of the Blackcap. And there is a very hard note of anger if the nesting site is approached. The birds move with great anxiety from perch to perch making a throaty sound: '*Surrer*'. A note of distress which is used when the parents are feeding young, but are not anxious to approach too near to the nest whilst under observation, is a sharp '*Tic*'.

By July the song is no more; we can only assume that somewhere low down in the shrubs or the deep tangle of the bramble the bird has its nest with us, for during the months of May and June the male bird sings constantly. Just where the nest is we do not know, and though I have an idea that it is in a certain wild corner I will not try to look, for I have no wish to attract Magpies. We must guess; we must hope that ours is one of the gardens where this fine songster has its home. It is, indeed, a well-loved visitor. In our village it is a common bird and I have found a number of nests in the hedges, one or two not too far apart, which was rather surprising as these birds are most jealous of their territory.

The nest is a very robust structure of grass, dead leaves and moss. I have noticed on more than one occasion that there was a good matting of hair in the interior. This was so well packed that I marvelled at the patience of the birds. All in all, the nest is a good cup of well-built material, in which the marbled beauty of the eggs is hidden.

The Garden Warbler feeds its young on live food that the gardener does not need, and thus renders him a service.

The Grasshopper Warbler

Locustella naevia

This bird's long-drawn-out, rising-and-falling, reedy song bears no resemblance, as far as I can detect, to the sounds made by any of the grasshoppers inhabiting Great Britain. Its rather puzzling name may conceivably derive from its skill in creeping inconspicuously through low undergrowth, appearing and disappearing as though it were an insect rather than a bird. Certainly the name has no connection with the bird's song, to which I used to listen again and again when one nested on a patch of marshy woodland some thirty yards from our house, and where it sang every day in early morning and at dusk.

The nearness of its nest gave me an excellent opportunity to memorize its song, which is a thin, reedy note prolonged for over three minutes. That is the timing I have, though it is quite possible that other birds can continue for even longer. Its performance is worth watching, for the bird is not shy if one remains still and quiet. It will turn its head from side to side, as if making sure that nobody misses any of it. The best description of the song is that it resembles a fisherman reeling in his line. The bird begins, after alighting on its chosen perch or platform, with '*Slirr - err - err - err - err - err - err - err - err - err - err*', continuing on and on, the rising and falling of the sound governed by the turning of its head.

At Purdis Heath just outside Ipswich there is an area of heathland owned by the Ipswich Golf Club. Through the kindness of the members, I have been able to spend many hours by the big lakes there. This is one of the places where I have been most fortunate in my observation of the Grasshopper Warbler. By one of the lakes a huge tree had fallen, and part of its trunk reached out over the water. It made an ideal song post for this strange small bird.

I remember early one morning being there, having arrived during the previous night in order to be at hand when the bird began its odd reeling song. The water of the lake was giving off a thin vapour, almost as if it was slowly coming to the boil. As I watched the bird began to sing. Whether or not because of the rippling water or the sounds of leaping fish, the song from this bird was very much like the reeling in of a fishing line by an unseen angler.

There are times when the bird shows signs of alarm and its song gives way to a short, sharp, thin note which sounds like '*Pick*'. This will be repeated if, for instance, a Kestrel flies overhead. Then we get '*Pick - pick - pick - pick*' in quick succession.

Near to Dunwich I have often sat near a piece of marshy ground overlooking the Minsmere bird sanctuary watching a Grasshopper Warbler moving like a mouse - or a grasshopper - through the undergrowth. Several birds, such as the Common Whitethroat, are skilful at moving through the lower growth of an untidy hedge, but the Grasshopper Warbler is an expert by comparison. The slender bird passes in and out of the undergrowth, appearing and then disappearing with apparently effortless ease. One may spot it for a moment as it pauses briefly to pick some unfortunate insect from beneath a leaf or blade of grass; then it disappears again.

We have never found any nests of the Grasshopper Warbler at Minsmere because they are obviously hidden with great care, and any efforts we made to find them would mean disturbing the undergrowth, and leaving a pathway for predators, both human and animal.

However, we have now become so used to the annual arrival of this slender bird, with its not very beautiful song, that we welcome it almost as warmly as we welcome the Chiffchaff. It no longer returns to the edge of the village where we were first introduced to it by some neighbours, for that has now been built on, but there is plenty of room for it in our own garden if it ever cares to nest there. And it will be most welcome.

94

RAYMOND WATSON

The Reed Warbler

Acrocephalus scirpaceus

I await with eagerness the arrival of this bird from its winter quarters, probably in East Africa. As I walk beside the brown heads of last year's reeds, watching them swaying like an inland sea of sepia waves, I hear the gentle voice of the Reed Warbler protesting that it has only just arrived, and is practising its song. It is a quiet little song, which one can easily miss, but it means, as the Cuckoo announces much more noisily, that 'summer is i-cumen in'. It can be heard first towards the end of April, and it continues until the end of July.

Compared with the hurried burst of song one gets from the Sedge Warbler, the muttered soliloquy of the Reed Warbler is gentleness itself. Unlike that of its noisy neighbour, however, it is easy to memorize, for it is a soft song lasting no more than four seconds.

If I stop to listen in the reed beds by riverside or lakeside, all I hear to begin with is a scratchy bedlam from two or three Sedge Warblers singing together. Then, probably because a mayfly has passed over the waving brown heads of the reeds, and the Sedge Warblers have leapt on fluttering wings to intercept it, the bedlam ceases. At that moment one can pick out the soft, self-effacing murmur of the Reed Warbler, mingled with the rustle of the wind through the reed heads. Its full song is enchanting. It has a clarity of notes which sound exactly like '*Cirruck, cirrack, cirruck, wilcock, wilcock, werk*', repeated time and again.

It is one of the most charming of riverside sounds, if you can distinguish it from the noisy sounds of the Sedge Warbler. Where there is a jungle of reeds it is a song that is as constant as the breeze. I have no notes of it singing later than the last week of July, but I have to confess that I have occasionally tried to encourage a Sedge Warbler to protest by dropping a clod of earth into the reeds, and have thereby startled a Reed Warbler into fitful song. It has an alarm note which sounds distinctly irritable, a deep note which will, if the intruder persists in staying around, become a prolonged burst: '*Sur - sur - sur*'.

Its food, as one might expect, consists largely of insects frequenting the reed beds or the waterside. One can observe the heads of the reeds swaying, and then a Reed Warbler will rise from amongst them to capture a hapless mayfly climbing up to adulthood on the broad stem of a yellow iris.

The nest is a most skilful exercise in weaving, using reed stems as scaffolding. I have watched by the hour the industrious little birds collecting dried grasses and stitching them in and out of the reed stems. They seem to have an instinctive knack of constructing a deep cup and then slinging it, hammock-like, between the firm stems of the reeds. The eggs are almost always a shade of green, mottled with dark markings. I have never found more than four to a nest.

One evening I was sitting in a watcher's hut when I saw a large bird swoop hawk-like over the reeds. It was greeted with a volley of alarm notes from the Warblers on all sides, for it was a Cuckoo looking for a nest in which to lay its egg. Though some fellow-ornithologists have told me that they have found Reed Warblers' nests vandalized, presumably by Cuckoos, I have to admit that although I have found Cuckoos' eggs in the nests of Robins, Dunnocks, Meadow Pipits and Chaffinches I have never found one in a Reed Warbler's nest.

When on the wing it is a little difficult to distinguish from the Sedge Warbler, though it lacks the latter's conspicuously streaked head and back. The Reed Warbler is acrobatic in its movements amongst the reeds, but is a rather shy creature, not nearly as bold as the Sedge Warbler. However often I heard its song, it seldom showed its head over the feathery brown tops of the reeds, as though too modest to show the listener who was responsible for a song consisting of only six or seven notes continuously repeated.

96

RAYMOND WATSON

The Sedge Warbler

Acrocephalus schoenobaenus

The Sedge Warbler has so many local names that it is evidently well known to country folk. These include 'Blethering Tam', 'Chittering Tam', 'Night Singer', 'Mock Bird', and 'Lesser Water Sparrow'. The name 'Night Singer' is a good one, for the Sedge Warbler will often sing during the night. Many times, while sitting in huts in a bird sanctuary, I have heard it breaking into song though it was quite dark. It seems that any sound which appears alien to this small bird will immediately be challenged with an outburst of irritable song.

During its hurried song it is often possible to hear odd imitations of other birds, especially some of their calls. There is a brook near my house where often I have sat on the bridge and listened with my eyes closed in order to be able to concentrate and identify the different imitations which would pour from the wide-open beak of the perched Sedge Warbler, for it would sing in full view. There was the stutter of the Redpoll; this was much favoured, but there was scarcely time to register one imitation before another followed it. There was the '*Weep - eep*' of the Yellow Wagtail, and in quick succession the hurried twitter which comes at the end of the song of a Swallow. Then, in passing, the abrupt '*Cur-ruch*' of the Waterhen, and at once, almost as a punctuation, the '*Chark*' of a Jackdaw, and the four notes of a Reed Bunting.

The Sedge Warbler sings and imitates without the slightest apparent interest, for the sounds pour out in quick succession. After such a bout the bird will, for no apparent reason, almost leap into the air in a sudden flutter, not unlike the darting upward flight of the common Whitethroat.

At times it will fly into the nearest tree and sing its own song, which is an extraordinary burst of harsh notes and some that are quite lovely. The full song, which I have written down many times, omitting the imitations, is almost always the same: '*Se - se - se - se - sak - sak - sak - sak - pittut - pittut - tut - tut - tut - tut - see - uk - see - uk - see - uk - see - uk*'. This is repeated at great length, and all the sounds are repeated many times.

The alarm notes, making it obvious that the hidden bird is not amused at being disturbed, are a series of dry '*Suck - suck - suck*' sounds which can be easily imitated by an almost human '*tutting*' though the bird does have the advantage of the dry whistle which the human '*tut*' lacks.

There is a sanctuary just outside Ipswich where I have spent many a long night in the hut recording the sounds of the various birds as they announced their arrival. One night I had been listening to the voice of a Water Rail, a relative of the Corncrake, who seemed to be under the impression that he had the same gifts as the Nightingale. He put up a most discordant performance which was first like a miniature pig squealing, then a deep burping sound, followed by a phrase that came out of the darkness as '*Queer - queer*'. It was the strangest song ever; but the earnestness of the hidden performer came over with comical emphasis. Every so often the Water Rail paused for breath and then a Sedge Warbler came in with its own version of 'A Night in the Reeds'. Finally these two birds joined in an incredible duet. I listened with rapt attention to this extraordinary performance.

I have read that the Sedge Warbler will always nest in the near vicinity of water; but I have on many occasions found the nest in rough hedges in a tangle of untidy weed, with no water within hundreds of yards. The nest is not the deep cup which the Reed Warbler builds; it is made of local materials, but if the site is near to water the materials are reed heads, feathers and grasses with the occasional addition of willow catkins. The eggs are settled in an untidy bulky nest; they are neat little ovals with a ground colour of buff and at times some streaks of thin dark lines. As to food, the bird is no problem in a garden, for its diet is of small slugs, worms and insects.

98

RAYMOND WATSON

The Willow Warbler

Phylloscopus trochilus

Most garden lovers will have their favourite garden bird, chiefly because of its voice. Some will rave about their Blackbird; others will tell you of their Robin, or their Thrush. These, of course, are resident birds, so we have ample opportunities of choosing favourites. During the summer season, also, we have superb singers from warmer countries, such as the Blackcap, Garden Warbler, Tree Pipit and Nightingale.

My favourite is the Willow Warbler, and I am sure anyone who knows the bird and its sweet descending notes will agree that it is a superb songster. True, it lacks the power of the more famous, but it soon becomes the dominant song in our gardens from its sheer persistence. Many times visitors to our home have said: 'What is the bird? I've never heard a song so often repeated'. This is true, for the Willow Warbler male will pour out, minute after minute, a succession of songs. I have counted as many as nine songs in a minute.

The outburst of songs is solely to make territorial claims. While the female is building the nest the male keeps up this torrent of song. He will usually perch at the top of a tree where he can keep an eye on what goes on around him. In this garden of mine I have a pair who have visited us each year, and during the past four years have done us the honour of building their nest with us. They choose the base of one of the silver birches where the grass is long and very rarely cut. The female builds the nest on her own, and it is a joy to peep at when she has finished. It is an igloo of moss, with an entrance hole at the side. I have watched her as she finished the interior. With her tail just protruding, she turns round and round, giving the finishing touches to a miniature marvel of architecture.

The eggs are usually laid between the first week and the second week of May. I well remember my wife's expression of wonderment when I gently pushed to one side the feathers which showed at the opening. There were five of the most beautiful works of nature that it was possible to see: white, covered with fine red spots. We didn't look again until the parents were feeding their young. Then we marvelled at the attention paid to the female by the male bird. He came down the birch tree, branch by branch, calling with a soft '*Toyee*' until he was just above the nest. Then his mate came out of her igloo, shivering her wings like a fledgling, and pleaded for food. He would pop small caterpillars into her wide-open beak, and then fly up into the tree and sing. The song is warbled down the scale and dies away into a murmur; if it is whispered you will have an excellent idea of the composition of the whole phrase: '*See – tit – tit – tit – tur – tur – bee – whip – ip – pie – whopit – tur – chee – oo*'.

When Cuckoos are hunting and calling I have heard a pair of Willow Warblers making sounds which I can only describe as a strange mixture of laughter and distress. The thin high-pitched notes make a very odd combination of sound: '*Sin – sin – sin – sin – sin – sin – sin – sin – ee – sin*'.

When I was working for the BBC Pebble Mill programme, we were recording the voices of the birds to be found by and on water in a Worcestershire river. My imitations had decoyed Canada Geese, Herons and other waterbirds when I noticed a pair of Willow Warblers across the water. They were calling to each other with plaintive cries of alarm, even though each appeared to be carrying in its beak a wriggling green caterpillar. This sight amused the producer of the programme, Derek Smith, who asked if I could persuade them to cross the river so that he could get a close-up picture of them. So I imitated a Cuckoo. This was almost too successful, for the Willow Warblers promptly flew across the river, to mob their supposed enemy, complaining bitterly with that sad call that sounds like laughter. Derek Smith got his picture, and some remarkable sound effects, too.

RAYMOND WATSON

The Wood Warbler

Phylloscopus sibilatrix

This lovely little Warbler is one of my favourites. When I was a boy I was told by local ornithologists that I would never hear this bird in Suffolk. I was delighted to discover one at Kesgrave near Ipswich when I was fourteen years old.

It was high up in a tree, and it was difficult to distinguish the greenish yellow of its underparts in the bright sunlight shining through the leaves. I was puzzled by it, not least because there appeared to be two different songs coming from the tree. I thought at first there must be two birds in the tree, but when one bird came into closer view, searching for food amongst the leaves, I realized that it was responsible for both songs. One was an elfin-like '*Pew – pew – pew – pew – pew – pew – pew*'. The other came at intervals, and was quite different, a clear opening burst of '*Stip – stip – stip – stip – stip – stip*', followed by a shrill '*Diter – ee – ee – ee – ee – ee – ee – ee – ee*', almost insect-like in its lack of any music.

The Wood Warbler is reputed to frequent tall trees in beech and oak woods, but while this may to some extent be true, both my wife and I have seen it singing and feeding at the top of not very tall hedges in Wales. True, there was a shortage of suitable trees in that area, but the bird did not seem in any way bothered by that. It fed almost exclusively on insects, and I have never watched a bird which had such a predilection for this kind of diet. I know that birds can change their diet owing to lack of what they like, but this one seemed to seek only insects, those hidden beneath leaves and those unwise enough to crawl about at the bottom of a hedge. During this period of bird-watching we noticed that it constantly called a soft '*Sue*'. Whether it was alarmed at our presence I do not know, but this did not seem to affect its appetite.

We also noticed that it sometimes left the hedges and flew short distances, singing in flight. There are a surprising number of wild birds which will sing when on the wing. I have heard Wrens, Blackbirds and even Song Thrushes do so, but usually this is due to a wish to claim territorial rights. Many birds also sing in the routine of courtship, but few can surpass the Wood Warbler for showmanship on these occasions. He will dart up into the air for all the world like a rising Sky Lark, but in a moment he is back again, ready to go through the movements once more. He is a superb artist in flight, using his wings as it seems no other can. The female, like so many others, makes a show of indifference, reacting only with a slight shiver of the wings, but as soon as the cock imagines he is welcome she will dash off at speed.

The nest is like those of other summer-visiting Warblers, such as the Chiffchaff and the Willow Warbler, for it is domed and has an entrance at the side. The use of bracken as a bulk is noticeable, and I suggest that this is why the nest is usually near to woodland, where bracken is plentiful and there are lots of suitable leaves available. It is the female who does all the nest-building. The eggs are much darker than those of other Warblers, heavily marked with dark brown, almost black, spots, which cannot be confused with those of the Chiffchaff or Willow Warbler.

At Hever in Kent, during broadcast recordings with Brian Johnston, we erected five microphones in places where we knew individual birds used to sing. During the actual broadcast, which in those days was live, we could switch over to any microphone as and when needed. One of these birds was a Wood Warbler who sang with exquisite clarity, and we were able to record it. The copse from which it sang was of hazel shrubs, and the picture was a delightful one, for the sunlight broke through the hazel leaves and dappled them with a soft light capturing the Wood Warbler in a ray of mellow light which so enhanced the yellow chin and throat of the bird that it was a great pity television was not available in those days.

The Whitethroat

Sylvia communis

'Old Scratchy' is our affectionate name for this bird, who visits our garden with regularity each year. It arrives about the middle of April and at once announces its arrival with outbursts of irritable song. I don't think I have ever heard a wild bird who sounds as bad-tempered as does this small warbler. Even if it is not singing it keeps up a dry alarm note as if to warn others 'Look out, watch that man; he is up to no good'. After a while you get the message, that you are not welcome in your own garden!

The bird also always seems to be in a hurry. It will leap up, fluttering its wings, and singing its scratchy song in fitful bursts as if the time spent in song was a task which it was compelled to undertake. One of the local names sums up very well the habit of this fussy creature: it is 'Singing Sky Rocket'. But I watch it daily, and never grow tired of listening as it rises up like a doubtful learner, in jerky wing flaps. Then without warning the song ends, and the bird drops like a stone into the hedge from which it rose. What is also amusing is that the bird, as soon as it drops, hides, and its song gives way to a bad-tempered slurring note. This note is a prolonged '*Chuurer*'. Another note which carries no welcome to the listener is '*Seck-seck*'. Then there is a series of notes which I find hard to explain for they are not so bad-tempered in tone as the others. They may be just contact calls, though the idea of this bird being amiable even to its own kind seems a bit far-fetched.

The song is short, scratchy and sung as if the bird were conveying to the listener, '*Aye - aye - that's the lot (tidder - er - bee - yer - beat - yer - bottet - chee)*'. At times it will make what seem to be attempts to polish the song and refine it, comical as this may seem, and the notes will be clear and even sweet. Seemingly overcome by its efforts the bird will dance overhead with curious abandon, and then, as if its faith in itself suddenly evaporates, it drops into the hedge and vanishes.

It makes its way through the tatty undergrowth of the ditch below the hedge with a skill that seems out of character for such a clumsy bird. It appears and vanishes time and again, scolding as it does so. It seems to love an untidy ditch, which is cluttered with dead twigs and leaves and a good growth of nettles. One local name for it is 'Nettle-Creeper'.

One year I had a pair of these excitable birds under observation for some time. They had nested low down in the bottom of a hedge, and their surroundings were really an appalling muddle. There was garden rubbish as well as rampant growth of weeds. Polypody fern vied with nettles and ground ivy to get a chance of seeing the light, whilst that incredibly hardy little plant known as Dog's Mercury stood around in ranks. Amongst this confusion the Whitethroats had built their nest. They had chosen a willow twig as a foundation, and somehow had anchored it solidly. Yet, had I not been in the top of a pollarded willow, and able to look straight down, I would have seen no indication that Whitethroat were at home.

I had used this willow on a number of occasions for watching Shelduck who had bored a hole in the bank, and I would not have seen the Whitethroats had they kept quiet. But a weasel came into view, like a tiny furred snake, and started searching in the tangled undergrowth. Instantly he was mobbed by the two birds, who proceeded to scold it with their slurred alarm notes. The weasel looked up at them and made a stuttering, abusive reply, but in so doing missed the nest. Maybe wild birds are wiser than we are prepared to admit.

The Common Whitethroat's nest is a much more solid job than its cousin, the Lesser Whitethroat, makes, for the foundation is a cup of solidly packed grass, in which the five eggs are laid. I have seen Whitethroat eggs that are greenish with brown markings, while in another clutch they were white with grey markings and red marks round the larger end.

RAYMOND WATSON

The Lesser Whitethroat

Sylvia curruca

The Lesser Whitethroat measures five and a quarter inches in total length. When considering the difference between the two Whitethroats, Shakespeare's comment on roses comes to mind: 'What's in a name?' In this case, a quarter of an inch.

My wife and I know this bird by the affectionate name of 'The Rattler'. It announces its arrival with a dry rattle of double notes which is very easy to recognize. The rattle lasts for only a few seconds, with increasing pauses between the notes.

For some years I thought that this rattle was all there was to the song. Then one day I was leaning over the pond, and watching the courtship antics of frogs, when I heard, in the big willow above me, a soft warble that was not unlike the irritable song of the Common Whitethroat. It continued, and then, to my astonishment, it was followed by the familiar rattle. So *that* was the complete song: '*Seepa - sit - it - it - ta*'. Then '*Chedda - chedda - chedda - chedda - chedda - chedda*'. The final part, being the 'rattle', can be heard from a fair distance, but the prelude, the '*Seepa - sit - it - it - ta*', can be heard only when one is close by.

Other notes, that are commonly given as an alarm, are a drying '*Sack - sack*' or just '*Sack*', which can be easily initiated by putting the first two fingers against one's mouth and making a kissing sound. The Lesser Whitethroat finds this irresistible, for, like its larger cousin, it is a very inquisitive bird.

It is an odd fact that the larger Whitethroat does not believe in hiding its light under a bushel, and will sing in full view, but the lesser bird is very shy and sings only when hidden. However, an imitation of its song will bring it out from its hiding place to seek its rival. I sing with it regularly as soon as it arrives, and we both get some much-needed practice.

As far as I am aware the Lesser Whitethroat has not nested in our garden, though it spends a lot of time treating us to its familiar rattle. I know where it does nest, and that is in a hedge adjoining our garden; so I hope that one day the offspring may spread their wings and come and nest with us. They would not only be welcome because of their song but also because of the good they would do in keeping the garden pests at bay.

One of the most interesting aspects of the study of bird behaviour is watching the kind of food a bird consumes or feeds to its young. It is only then that one realizes the immense numbers of agricultural pests they account for. Even if a pair of birds has only one brood during a season it means that for one or two months the appetites of five or six young birds have to be satisfied, and this almost entirely from insects and other pests that are destructive to vegetation.

If one turns over old tree stumps one will almost always unearth quantities of wireworms, small larvae and other creepy-crawlies. Before one has walked more than a few paces away one will see Lesser Whitethroats descending on them, picking them up and carrying them off to their young. If one disturbs an ants' nest the birds will decimate the panic-stricken hoards of ants. They are adept at locating and eliminating all kinds of insect pests that plague raspberry, gooseberry and blackberry plants.

I remember one day noticing what I took to be some unusual bristling of the slim branches of a willow tree in our garden, and while I was wondering what had caused it, a Whitethroat flew into the tree and began to peck at the bristling. Later I looked more closely and saw the bristlings were caused by massed ranks of grey aphides. The bird and its mate came back again and again, collecting them and taking them to the young in their nest. If it were not for benefactors like this half the trees would be denuded of their green leaves. Mr and Mrs Rattler are therefore very welcome in our garden.

106

RAYMOND WATSON

The Wren

Troglodytes troglodytes

One of the oldest country sayings is: 'You will never catch a weasel asleep'. How true! But this bright-eyed little highwayman of our hedgerows is not the only one who is alert. There is one small bird, the Wren, whose claim to needle-sharp alertness is equal to that of the weasel. You have only to watch one feeding: it will pick and look, pick and look; constant vigil keeps it alive. Over the past years, walking the countryside during both darkness and daylight, I have never found a Wren idle, and certainly not asleep. Any sound I may have made was at once recorded, and a sharp note of annoyance told me that the Wren was fully aware of my presence.

The male Wren is a compulsive nest builder. He makes what are known as cock's nests. The female is led in triumph to each until she decides to accept one; then she completes the interior. The complete nest is as snug an example of home-making as you will find. It is a ball of leaves on the outside, with an inner wall of moss, lined with softer materials. The entrance hole is just large enough to admit a human finger. It rises up from the opening to the perfect hollow of the egg chamber, which is a work of art constructed with the tiny architect using only its beak and its breast. The latter is used to make the egg chamber round. The eggs are tiny and white, faintly spotted with red, normally about seven in number.

I buy coconuts and saw an inch from one end, leaving a hole about an inch in diameter. This I hang up for the benefit of the hungry Titmice, who soon clean the white meat from the interior. When all has been consumed I wedge the coconut in amongst some ivy and the rambler rose which climbs a fence and hangs down over the ivy like a dark green shawl. Within two days a Wren will have found it, and a snug wall of moss will have been welded round the inside of the coconut,

with just the hollow left. I now have six coconut shell homes for Wrens, planted round the garden. In the winter I put a small quantity of a soft food just inside the shell, for in a hard winter Wrens suffer severely.

Vocally the Wren is a mighty atom. It is the untrained tenor of our gardens. For at least ten months of the year a bright, hurried burst of shrill song comes to us, from the top of the ivy, with tail cocked, beak wide open, and the bird's tiny body quivering.

If you whisper the following notes, making a kind of sibilant of each one, bearing in mind that the whole song is shrill, and lasts but five seconds, you will have an excellent idea of the song and its make-up of notes: '*Weet - teet - stip - stip - stip - stip - stip - tit - tit - tit - tit - tit - tit - ter - er - er - er - swee - ee - chip - chip - chip - chip - wet*'. The first two notes are deliberate and clear. The next five are hurried but distinct. Then the following six notes very quick, followed by the '*ter - er - er*'. Almost reedy these are. Then the deliberate '*Swee - ip - chip - chip - chip - chip - wet*', challenging, defiant finish.

From February to July the song increases in volume and is sung at the rate of five times in a minute. Under stress or rivalry it can be almost continuous. The alarm notes can be varied, for example an abrupt '*Sit - it*' or a prolonged reedy burst, like a short impression of the Grasshopper Warbler's song: '*Ter - er - er - er - er - er - er*'. The short notes are rattled in a continuing phrase, like a finger nail across the teeth of a comb. There is also almost a '*tutting*' note, like an irritable human.

The Wren is a friend of the gardener. It destroys weevils, spiders and the larvae of moths and butterflies, as well as harmful pests of vegetation. Its size is very small: three and a half inches from beak to tail. I have a fellow feeling for the Wren, for I am only five feet six inches in height. The Wren compensates for its size by having a voice that can be heard from a considerable distance. Perhaps that is one reason why I have spent much of my life learning to whistle.

The Yellowhammer

Emberiza citrinella

This is amongst the most gorgeous of our wild birds. Often the sight of one rising and swooping ahead of us as we walk along a country lane is a bit of a puzzle, for the tawny gold of its head and the orange of its rump might lead us into thinking that a Canary has escaped and was enjoying its brief freedom. Rising and swooping is an accurate description of its very individual habit of flight.

A Yellowhammer in a gorse patch is a sight not easily forgotten, with the gold clusters of blossom and the rich gold of the bird's head and breast as he lifts his head to din out that endless little song, a song which has for years been known as 'a little bit of bread and no-oo-cheese'. The song can vary, however, for I have heard an individual singing with slow deliberation, so that the notes were spaced out in a more leisurely way. The usual duration of the familiar phrase is but three seconds at the most, but on a close hot day, after the noon sun has passed over, the bird will perch on the end of a twig in a hedgerow and, crouching down on its legs, it will sing the ditty over and over again, almost with an air of boredom.

There is a flight note that can be heard throughout the year, a double note which sounds like '*Sil - ip*'. And there is another which is offered from a hedge when it seems that the bird is telling all who will listen that he is at home and in full command. This note has a metallic sound, '*Zint*'. There is also an alarm note which is very abrupt, as if the Yellowhammer had been surprised by an intruder and had no time to do other than utter a '*Twit*' and then dart away in quick flight.

The courtship performance of the male Yellowhammer has to be seen to be believed. All male birds display during the mating season, but I doubt whether I have ever seen a more colourful performance than one I watched the other day. The female appeared to be not in the least interested, but this did not deter the handsome fellow. He first bent his head as if in modesty, but then he dazzled the eye with a wealth of colour, especially on his rump and his wide-spread tail. This bout of showing off had an almost human arrogance, as if this male Yellowhammer were saying, 'Look well, girl; you have never seen the like of this before'. I was a good distance away, and I watched through my field glasses, but I had to admit that if conceit was at the back of all this display he had reason for it. His breast, his glorious head and his rump were tawny gold. Truly a superbly endowed creature.

So far this bird and his mate have not nested with us. I have, of course, found nests farther away, in gorse thickets and on wayside banks. The nest is a neat cup of teased-out grasses and oddments of animal hair. There is a base of moss which is neatly woven into the sides and the interior, providing a snug retreat for the three eggs. It may seem strange but I have never found more than three eggs in a Yellowhammer's nest. They are lovely eggs, for the shell colour is a washed purple and white, with the strangest markings and lines, and a deep cluster of dark markings at the larger end.

These birds will produce at least two broods in a season which begins early in May. I have read that at times they will rear three broods, and I am sure that this is quite possible, especially when an early session begins in April. The song begins in February and can be heard all through until early September.

Such a handsome creature inevitably attracts many local names, for country folk have always been ready to devise their own pet names for birds which have conspicuous characteristics, as the Yellowhammer undoubtedly does. Its correct name, however, is derived from 'Ammer', which is the German name for a Bunting. But the local names to be found in different parts of Britain include 'Yellow Yeldrock', 'Yellow Yite', 'Yellow Yowley', 'Goldie', 'Goldspink', 'Golden Gladdy', and 'Scotch Canary'.

RAYMOND WATSON

INDEX